Lebanese Cuisine

THE AUTHENTIC COOKBOOK

Lebanese Cuisine

THE AUTHENTIC COOKBOOK

SAMIRA KAZAN

Publisher Mike Sanders
Art Director William Thomas
Senior Editor Alexandra Andrzejewski
Senior Designer Jessica Lee
Photographer, Chef, & Stylist Samira Kazan
Recipe Testers Ashley Brooks, Lovoni Walker
Proofreader Lisa Starnes
Indexer Brad Herriman

First American Edition, 2022
Published in the United States by DK Publishing
6081 E. 82nd Street, Indianapolis, IN 46250

Published in the United States
by Dorling Kindersley Limited.

A Library of Congress catalog number is available
upon request.
ISBN: 978-0-7440-5449-1

DK books are available at special discounts when
purchased in bulk for sales promotions, premiums,
fundraising, or educational use. For details, contact:
SpecialSales@dk.com

Printed and bound in China

For the curious
www.dk.com

Contents

CHICKEN & FISH

BARBECUE

VEGETARIAN

Desserts & Beverages

Staples

Introduction

I am Samira, but I am better known as Alphafoodie. If you had a look through my social media or blog (ALPHAFOODIE.COM), you would see that I share creative, healthy recipes that encompass my love for colorful, mostly plant-based, natural food and my passion for making everything from scratch. I am originally Lebanese, and I often put a Lebanese spin on dishes.

I was born and raised in Lebanon, a charming Mediterranean country and home to the oldest city in the world, Byblos. I grew up in a large family where dinner was quality time spent together and everyone gathered at the table, sharing, laughing, and enjoying. I remember the long hours my mom would spend in the kitchen cooking delicious food. She always looked so serene, selecting herbs, chopping ingredients, tasting dishes, and smiling over what she made. And the family could tell how much love she poured into the food she served us. One of my earliest memories is enjoying my mom's freshly made Markouk flatbread. I recall my sisters and I, even at very young ages, would help her a lot in the kitchen. When the bread was ready, Mom would sit us down and we would enjoy the warm Markouk together.

Part of my love for food comes from my mom. She taught me how to select the best ingredients, how to use them, and how to preserve them. She introduced me not only to traditional recipes but also to traditional ways of preserving our food—curing, fermenting, and jam-making. As I grew up and spent time living around the world, I kept those recipes close to my heart. Whenever I felt homesick, I'd make a batch of my favorite Lebanese food.

Living away from my family meant I had to learn to prepare and cook all my food by myself. At times, I'd ask my mom for tips on how best to create a dish; at times, I'd talk to other experienced Lebanese chefs. I wanted to know the best and most authentic way to make the recipes so they could be perfect, and so my mom would be proud of what I'd prepared. As I kept making my favorite recipes over and over again, I fell in love with cooking.

I love cooking all sorts of dishes—sweet, savory, spicy, and sour—and I enjoy sharing my dishes with others. I've shared dishes from cuisines around the world on my blog during the past few years, and I've always wanted to create something special with my Lebanese heritage.

Now, with this book, I'm sharing my experience with the world. I am so happy I could put together this collection of the most popular authentic Lebanese dishes. The book you are holding is the best of Lebanese cuisine.

I really do love Lebanese food. It's healthy, based on aromatic spices, earthy flavors, thin breads, whole grains, fresh vegetables, grilled meat, flavorful mezze appetizers, comforting dishes, and divine desserts. I find it's a joy to make—and eat, too!

Giving and sharing with those close to you is very much embedded in Lebanese culture. I share what I make nearly every day with friends or neighbors. Lebanese people also know how to celebrate life—and yes, you probably guessed it, it usually involves food! I feel like creating this book is an homage to this way of living.

There's an old saying in my village: the real secret to being a good cook is to love everything you do. For me, the essence of good food is ensuring love is a staple ingredient in my cooking.

This book is dedicated to my mother. I'm so grateful to her that she shared her tips, tricks, and all her love and care with me.

I hope you love these recipes as much as I do!

—Samira Kazan

A Distinct Culture of Food

Lebanese cuisine invites an unhurried pace with its many layered courses and hospitality mentality. From breakfast to dessert, the recipes in this book help you re-create traditional Lebanese meals at home. Breakfasts, whether quick weekday-morning meals or relaxed weekend fare, are nutritious dishes designed to fuel you through your morning. Mezze represent many of the hallmarks of Lebanese fare, like Fattoush, Moutbal (Eggplant Dip), and Warak Enab (Stuffed Grape Leaves). Similar to Spanish tapas, these shareable dishes are meant to be long-savored appetizers before the variety of mains and desserts are served. Mains are usually hearty, bright, and perfectly spiced dishes that feature lamb, fresh vegetables, grains, and legumes. Pita bread, rice, herbed salads, flavorful sauces, and pickles are mainstays on the Lebanese table to be enjoyed with all dishes. Finally, rich desserts like Qatayef (Sweet Pancakes with Cream or Nuts) are popular on holidays and special occasions, and fresh beverages such as Rose Lemonade are always welcome offerings.

Lebanese cuisine is vegan friendly, and most nonvegan recipes work well with plant-based meat alternatives. Instead of chicken, try this book's Vegan Chicken (Seitan), oyster mushrooms, or tofu—tofu skin is great for chicken drumsticks. Jackfruit and tempeh are good red meat replacements. For fish, try banana flower, heart of palm, lion's mane or trumpet mushrooms, or tofu, and season with nori or kelp for a "fishy" flavor. For minced meat, try crumbled tofu; this book's Soy Mince; or lentils, mushroom, or walnut mince—excellent for vegan kibbet.

Traditional or plant-based, there's no one right way to enjoy Lebanese cuisine. Choose a few recipes that look good, prepare enough to share with friends and family, and spend as much quality time together at the table as you like, enjoying the food and the company!

Breakfast

Manakish

BREAKFAST PIES

| PREP TIME: **20 MINUTES** | COOK TIME: **10 MINUTES** | TOTAL TIME: **30 MINUTES** |

MAKES: 3 za'atar manakish, 2 kishik manakish, & 1 cheese manakish

Manakish is a traditional Lebanese flatbread, similar to pizza. This bread is tasty for breakfast but also can be served as a snack, as an appetizer, or for brunch with your choice of toppings.

ingredients:

1 batch **Al Ajeen (Basic Dough; page 232)**

ZA'ATAR MANAKISH:

½ cup (50g) **Za'atar (Wild Oregano Mix; page 260)**

¼ cup (60ml) olive oil

3 balls Al Ajeen dough

KISHIK MANAKISH:

½ cup (60g) **Kishik (Powdered Fermented Yogurt & Wheat; page 256)**

2 medium tomatoes (198g), chopped

1 small yellow onion (125g), chopped

5 tbsp olive oil

½ tsp salt

½ tsp red chili powder

1 tsp sesame seeds

2 balls Al Ajeen dough

CHEESE MANAKISH:

½ cup (50g) Akkawi cheese, grated

½ cup (50g) shredded mozzarella

1 tsp nigella seeds

1 ball Al Ajeen dough

MAKE THE ZA'ATAR TOPPING:

Mix the Za'atar and olive oil until you get a paste.

MAKE THE KISHIK TOPPING:

In a mixing bowl, combine the Kishik, tomatoes, onion, olive oil, salt, chili powder, and sesame seeds.

MAKE THE CHEESE TOPPING:

If the Akkawi is salty, soak it in water for a few hours to remove the extra salt. Drain it well, and mix it with the mozzarella and nigella seeds.

MAKE THE MANAKISH (MANAKEESH):

1. Divide the dough into 6 balls (about 130g each).

2. Preheat the oven to 400°F (200°C).

3. Roll out 1 dough ball on a floured surface so it is quite thin and about 10 inches (25cm) in diameter. Top with some of the Za'atar-oil blend, Kishik, or cheese. Repeat with the remaining dough and toppings.

4. Transfer the bread to a baking sheet, and bake for 10 minutes or until lightly golden brown. Do not let the spices burn.

5. Remove the manakish from the oven, and enjoy with tomatoes, cucumber, mint, olives, and a cup of tea.

Fatayer Sabanekh

SPINACH PIES

PREP TIME: **20 MINUTES**	COOK TIME: **20 MINUTES**	TOTAL TIME: **40 MINUTES**

MAKES: 40 small pies

VEGAN

These savory spinach pastries are fresh, flavorful, and a delicious way to start your day. They're a staple on Lebanese breakfast tables.

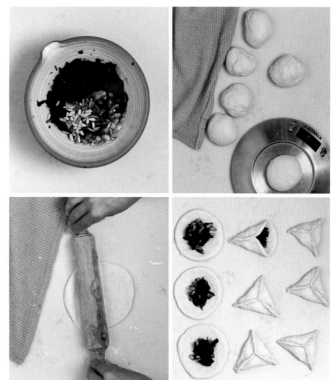

ingredients:

1 lb (450g) fresh spinach, chopped

2 tsp salt

1 small red or yellow onion (125g), diced small

2 tbsp toasted pine nuts (optional)

2 tbsp olive oil

2 tbsp freshly squeezed lemon juice

1 tbsp ground sumac

1 tbsp **Debs al Romman (Pomegranate Molasses; page 253)**

3 tbsp vegetable oil, plus more for greasing

1 batch **Al Ajeen (Basic Dough; page 232)**

storage:

Store in an airtight container in the refrigerator for up to 1 week, or freeze for 2 or 3 months.

1. Place the spinach in a bowl, rub with salt, and set aside to wilt and release its liquid. After 10 to 15 minutes, squeeze the spinach to remove as much of the liquid as possible, and return the spinach to the empty bowl.

2. To the spinach, add the onion, toasted pine nuts (if using), olive oil, lemon juice, sumac, and Debs al Romman, and mix well.

3. Preheat the oven to 350°F (180°C), and grease a baking sheet with some vegetable oil. Divide the dough into 40 small balls (about 20g each), and roll into thin circles about 4 inches (10cm) in diameter and ⅛ inch (3mm) thick.

4. Add 1 scant tablespoon spinach filling to each circle. Fold into a triangular shape by pinching two sides together, bringing the third side up to the center, and pinching closed.

5. Brush each pie with vegetable oil, arrange in a single layer on the prepared baking sheet, and bake for 15 to 20 minutes or until golden brown.

6. Enjoy with Laban Ayran (Salted Yogurt Drink; page 219).

Labneh

STRAINED YOGURT

PREP TIME: **6–12 HOURS**	COOK TIME: **NONE**	TOTAL TIME: **6–12 HOURS**

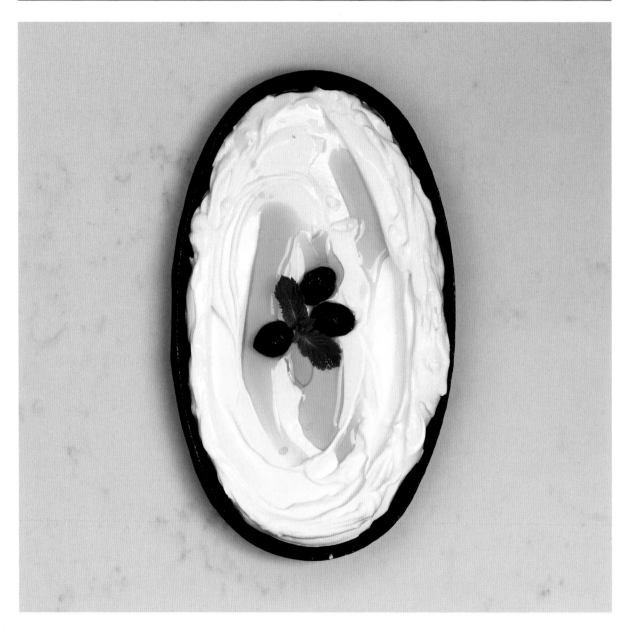

SERVES: 6

VEGAN (substitute almond or soy yogurt)

GLUTEN FREE

Labneh is an essential part of any Lebanese breakfast. This creamy Middle Eastern yogurt can be served as a dip with veggies or as a spread for Markouk (Paper Thin Bread; page 238) or pita bread. The ingredients are simple, and the preparation is easy.

ingredients:

4½ lb (2kg) plain full-fat
  yogurt

1 tsp salt

TO SERVE:

Extra-virgin olive oil

**Markouk (Paper Thin
  Bread; page 238) or**
pita bread

Olives

Fresh vegetables

storage:

Store in an airtight
glass container in
the refrigerator for
up to 5 days.

1. In a large bowl, mix the yogurt and salt.

2. Pour the yogurt into a cotton bag, hang over a
   deep bowl, and allow the liquid to strain for at least
   6 hours or overnight in the refrigerator (or at room
   temperature if it's not too warm). The longer you
   let it strain, the thicker the Labneh will be.

3. To serve, spread the Labneh in a bowl, and top with
   extra-virgin olive oil. Serve with Markouk or pita
   bread, olives, and fresh vegetables.

Foul Mudammas

FAVA BEANS

PREP TIME: **5 MINUTES**	COOK TIME: **1 HOUR**	TOTAL TIME: **1 HOUR 5 MINUTES**
+ overnight (soaking)		+ soaking

SERVES: 4

VEGAN

GLUTEN FREE (omit pita)

Start your day with this warm and comforting bean and vegetable breakfast dish, and you'll have the nutritional fuel to power you through your whole morning.

ingredients:

2½ cups (500g) dried fava beans

1 tsp baking soda

1 tsp salt, divided

1 bay leaf

1 tsp ground cumin

¼ tsp red chili powder (optional)

2 cloves garlic, peeled and crushed

Juice of 1 large lemon

TO SERVE:

Fresh flat-leaf parsley, chopped

Fresh mint leaves, chopped

Chopped tomatoes

⅓ cup (75ml) extra-virgin olive oil

Onions, radishes, turnips, peppers, pickles, olives

Pita bread

storage:

Store in an airtight container in the refrigerator for up to 1 week. Or omit the garlic, lemon juice, oil, and veggies, and freeze for up to 3 months.

variation:

You can use precooked or canned fava beans instead of dried. If using cooked, reheat 4 cups (840g) beans for 10 minutes before continuing with step 3. If using canned, skip steps 1 and 2. Rinse and drain the beans, and add, with ½ cup (125ml) water per can, to a pan, set over medium heat, and cook for 10 minutes. Turn off the heat, and smash the beans a little. Add just a pinch of salt, the cumin, chili powder (if using), garlic, and lemon juice, and mix well. Serve as directed.

1. In a large bowl, place the fava beans in water to cover, add the baking soda, and leave overnight to soak. (The beans will expand in size, so choose a large bowl.) Discard the soaking water, and wash the beans well. Place the beans in a large pot, and add plenty of water. Set over medium-high heat, and bring to a boil, skimming off the white foam as the beans cook.

2. Add ½ teaspoon salt and the bay leaf, cover partway (not completely), and simmer for about 1 hour. Remove and discard the bay leaf.

3. Pour the cooked beans in a deep bowl, and smash them a little using a fork. Add the cumin, chili powder (if using), garlic, remaining ½ teaspoon salt, and lemon juice, and mix well.

4. Spoon into small bowls. Top with parsley, mint, and tomatoes. Add a generous drizzle of extra-virgin olive oil, and serve with veggies and pita bread.

Balila

CHICKPEA BREAKFAST

PREP TIME: **15 MINUTES** + overnight (soaking)	COOK TIME: **1 HOUR**	TOTAL TIME: **1 HOUR 15 MINUTES** + soaking

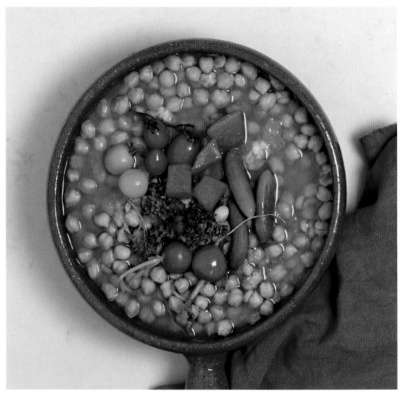

SERVES: 2

VEGAN

GLUTEN FREE

ingredients:

1 cup (208g) dried chickpeas

1 tsp baking soda

5 cups (1.2 liters) water, plus more
 for soaking

2 tsp salt, divided

1 tsp ground cumin

2 cloves garlic, peeled and crushed

Juice of 1 large lemon

TO SERVE:

2 tbsp chopped fresh flat-leaf parsley

½ tsp red chili powder

½ cup (125ml) extra-virgin olive oil

Fresh mint leaves

Tomatoes, radishes, onions, cucumber
 or turnip **Kabis (Pickles; page 246)**,
 peppers

A simple yet popular traditional breakfast dish, Balila is warm,
comforting, and full of rich and earthy flavors.

1. In a large bowl, soak the chickpeas and baking soda in water
   overnight. Drain and wash the chickpeas, and place in a large pot.
   Add the water, and bring to a boil over medium-high heat, skimming
   off any foam as they cook. Add 1 teaspoon salt, cover, and simmer
   for 1 hour. Alternatively, cook for 20 minutes in a pressure cooker.

2. Pour the warm chickpeas into a deep bowl, and smash them a little
   with a fork. Add the cumin, garlic, remaining 1 teaspoon salt, and
   lemon juice, and mix well.

3. Spoon into small bowls. Top with parsley; sprinkle with chili
   powder; add a generous drizzle of extra-virgin olive oil; and
   serve with fresh mint, veggies, and Kabis. Enjoy with pita bread.

Baid bil Awarma

MEAT PRESERVE WITH EGGS

PREP TIME: **NONE**	COOK TIME: **5 MINUTES**	TOTAL TIME: **5 MINUTES**

SERVES: 1

GLUTEN FREE

ingredients:

¼ cup (21g) **Awarma (Meat Preserve; page 249)**

2 eggs

With just two ingredients, this egg breakfast with a farm-style twist comes together quickly and easily (especially if you already have Awarma on hand)—perfect for busy weekday mornings.

1. In a frying pan over medium-high heat, heat the Awarma meat.

2. Reduce the heat to medium-low. Crack the eggs into a small bowl and whisk. Pour the eggs over the Awarma, and fry, stirring occasionally with a spatula, for 5 minutes.

3. Serve hot. Enjoy with pita bread or tucked into a sandwich.

Ejjeh

HERB OMELET

SERVES: 2

These savory egg, vegetable, and herb omelets are lightly fried until the edges are crispy and delicious. They're great for breakfast or as a light lunch.

ingredients:

5 small or 1 large
zucchini (325g)

1 tsp salt, divided

3 eggs

½ cup (60g) all-purpose
flour

1 bunch (53g) fresh flat-
leaf parsley, finely
chopped

6 green onions (10g),
finely chopped

¼ tsp black pepper
(optional)

¼ tsp ground allspice

3 tbsp olive oil

note:

Some people deep-fry
Ejjeh, but I prefer this
healthier panfried option.

variation:

Another southern
Lebanese way to make an
omelet is by combining 2
beaten eggs, ¼ cup (10g)
chopped fresh dill, a
sprinkle of salt and black
pepper, and 2 tablespoons
extra-virgin olive oil, and
baking on a baking sheet in
a preheated 350°F (180°C)
oven for 10 minutes.

1. Grate the zucchini, sprinkle with ½ teaspoon salt to remove excess water, and set it aside on a paper towel or in a strainer to drain.

2. Crack the eggs into a large mixing bowl and beat.

3. Add the flour, and whisk well.

4. Add the parsley, onions, remaining ½ teaspoon salt, pepper (if using), and allspice to the eggs, and stir to combine.

5. In a nonstick pan over medium-low heat, heat the olive oil.

6. Scoop about ¼ cup (150g) egg mixture into the pan, form into a circle, and cook for about 2 minutes. Flip the omelet over, and cook the other side for 2 more minutes.

7. Transfer the omelet to a plate, repeat with the remaining egg mixture, and serve warm.

Bayd b Banadoura

EGGS WITH TOMATO

| PREP TIME: **5 MINUTES** | COOK TIME: **15 MINUTES** | TOTAL TIME: **20 MINUTES** |

SERVES: 3

GLUTEN FREE (omit pita)

ingredients:

2 tbsp olive oil

½ cup (370g) chopped cherry tomatoes, or regular tomatoes

½ tsp salt

3 eggs

¼ tsp black pepper

¼ tsp red chili powder (optional)

Fresh oregano, thyme, basil, or your choice fresh herb

This classic egg breakfast balances a punch of protein with the fresh flavors of tomatoes and herbs.

1. In a skillet over medium-low heat, heat the olive oil. Add the cherry tomatoes, sprinkle with salt, cover, and cook for 10 minutes.

2. Smash the sautéed tomatoes in the skillet using a potato masher.

3. Crack the eggs one at a time, and drop them into the tomatoes, taking care not to break the yolks. Cover, and cook for 3 to 5 minutes or until the eggs are cooked to the consistency you prefer.

4. Season with black pepper and chili powder (if using).

5. Serve with your choice of fresh herbs—I used oregano. Enjoy with pita bread.

Kishik Soup

SERVES: 2

ingredients:

3 tbsp extra-virgin olive oil, divided

1 small yellow onion (87g), finely chopped

⅓ cup (43g) **Kishik (Powdered Fermented Yogurt & Wheat; page 256)**

1 cup (250ml) cold water

Fresh oregano or your choice fresh herb

Markouk (Paper Thin Bread; page 238) or pita bread

storage:

Store in an airtight container in the refrigerator for up to 3 days. If the soup thickens, add a bit of water when you warm it.

note:

When adding water in step 3, be sure to use cold water. Do not use warm water, which will result in clumps.

Kishik, traditionally made with dried bulgur wheat and yogurt, is a staple in Lebanese pantries. Once you have the yogurt-wheat powder, this healthy breakfast soup comes together quickly.

1. In a saucepan over medium-low heat, heat 2 tablespoons olive oil. Add the onion, and sauté for about 2 or 3 minutes or until the onion is golden.

2. Add the Kishik, and cook, stirring constantly, for 1 minute.

3. Add the cold water, stir well, and simmer for about 5 minutes or until the mixture starts boiling and thickens.

4. Serve hot, garnished with the remaining 1 tablespoon olive oil and oregano or your choice of fresh herb, with Markouk or pita bread.

Mezze

Tabbouleh

| PREP TIME: **10 MINUTES** | COOK TIME: **NONE** | TOTAL TIME: **10 MINUTES** |

SERVES: 3
VEGAN

This fresh Levantine salad is a very popular side dish on Mediterranean menus and is served as part of the traditional Lebanese mezze. Enjoy Tabbouleh with lettuce, grape, or cabbage leaves.

ingredients:

3 green onions (47g), diced small

2 medium ripe tomatoes (1½ cups/287g), chopped small

3 cups (185g) fresh flat-leaf parsley, finely chopped

⅓ cup (10g) fresh mint leaves, finely chopped

1 romaine lettuce heart (about 130g), leaves separated

DRESSING:

Juice of 2 medium lemons

2½ tbsp bulgur wheat

½ cup (125ml) extra-virgin olive oil

½ tsp salt

¼ tsp black pepper

storage:

Tabbouleh is best eaten fresh, but it can be stored in an airtight container in the refrigerator for up to 3 days.

notes:

Wash the herbs and vegetables and dry them very well. You don't want any extra moisture in the salad.

Also, don't chop the herbs in a food processor. Chop them by hand for the best texture.

1. Prepare the dressing. In a small bowl, combine the lemon juice, bulgur wheat, olive oil, salt, and pepper. Set aside so the bulgur wheat can soften and absorb the liquid.

2. In a large bowl, mix together the onions, tomatoes, parsley, and mint.

3. Add the dressing and bulgur wheat to the vegetables, stir to combine, and serve with romaine leaves.

Fattoush

SERVES: 4
VEGAN

This traditional Lebanese salad is one of my favorites. Made with a mixture of salad vegetables, toasted pita bread, and a delicious pomegranate salad dressing, it's a quick and healthy appetizer, side, or main dish.

ingredients:

1 pita bread (about
1½ cups/42g pieces)

1 romaine lettuce head
(about 317g), chopped

¾ lb (340g) medium
tomatoes or cherry
tomatoes, chopped

2 small cucumbers
(about 224g),
chopped

½ cup (57g) radishes,
sliced

½ cup (10g) fresh mint
leaves, chopped

1 cup (28g) fresh flat-
leaf parsley, chopped

2 green onions (32g),
chopped

⅓ cup (54g)
pomegranate seeds

1 tsp ground sumac

DRESSING:

2 tbsp freshly squeezed
lemon juice

2 tbsp extra-virgin olive
oil

1½ tbsp **Debs al
Romman
(Pomegranate
Molasses; page 253)**

2 cloves garlic, diced or
minced

½ tsp salt

1. Preheat the oven to 350°F (180°C). Cut the pita into
   bite-sized pieces, and separate into single layers.
   Arrange the pieces on a baking sheet, and toast for 12
   minutes or until brown and crispy. Don't let them burn.

2. In a large bowl, toss together the lettuce, tomatoes,
   cucumbers, radishes, mint, parsley, and green onions.

3. Prepare the dressing. In a small bowl, mix together the
   lemon juice, olive oil, Debs al Romman, garlic, and salt.
   Pour the dressing over the salad, and mix well.

4. Add the toasted pita bread and pomegranate seeds,
   sprinkle the sumac over the top, and serve.

storage:

Store for up to 2 days in the refrigerator. If you want to make
the salad ahead of time, leave out the pita, radishes, and dressing,
and add them just before serving. Store the dressing in a sealed jar
or glass bottle in the refrigerator for up to 1 week.

notes:

Traditionally, the pita bread is deep-fried, but you can toast
it in the oven instead and the recipe will still taste great.

Red bell peppers or other mixed peppers would be a great
addition to this salad, too.

Hummus bi Tahini

HUMMUS

PREP TIME: **5 MINUTES**	COOK TIME: **NONE**	TOTAL TIME: **5 MINUTES**

SERVES: 4

VEGAN

GLUTEN FREE

This is a simple recipe for a rich, creamy, delicious hummus. The velvety spread is perfect on pita bread or served with crunchy fresh veggies for dipping. Hummus is traditionally used in mezze meals and is a staple side for grilled meat and mashawi.

1. In a blender, purée the chickpeas, garlic, salt, lemon juice, Taratur, and ½ cup (125ml) chickpea liquid (aquafaba) or iced water, until smooth. If the consistency is too thick, add more liquid, blending until you reach the desired consistency.

2. Spread the hummus in a serving bowl, and add a generous drizzle of extra-virgin olive oil (if using). Serve with fresh vegetables. Enjoy with pita bread.

ingredients:

3 cups (594g) cooked chickpeas, or 2 (15 oz/ 425g) cans chickpeas, drained and liquid (aquafaba) reserved

3 cloves garlic

½ tsp salt

¼ cup (60ml) freshly squeezed lemon juice

½ cup (125ml) **Taratur** (Tahini Sauce; page 251)

1 cup (250ml) aquafaba or iced water (see note), divided

2 tbsp extra-virgin olive oil (optional)

Fresh vegetables

storage:

Store in an airtight container in the refrigerator for up to 4 or 5 days, or freeze for up to 4 to 6 months.

notes:

Aquafaba is the cooking water or liquid from the can from the chickpeas. You can adjust the hummus texture to your preference by adding more or less aquafaba.

Iced water can balance any heat produced by the blending.

variations:

Hummus Awarma: Sprinkle fried **Awarma (Meat Preserve; page 249)** on top.

Hummus Beiruti: Garnish with chopped fresh flat-leaf parsley, add a few chickpeas to the center, sprinkle with red chili powder, and top with a generous drizzle of extra-virgin olive oil.

Batata Harra

SPICY POTATOES

PREP TIME: **10 MINUTES**	COOK TIME: **35 MINUTES**	TOTAL TIME: **45 MINUTES**

SERVES: 4

VEGAN

GLUTEN FREE

These simple, healthy, spicy Lebanese potatoes, made with chili pepper, garlic, cilantro, and lemon juice, are great as a side or a main dish. Extra lemon juice on top gives these naturally vegan and gluten-free potatoes an extra zing!

ingredients:

4 medium russet potatoes (about 2 lb/ 962g), peeled and cubed

Vegetable oil, for deep-frying, or 1 tbsp extra-virgin olive oil, for baking and air-frying

1 tbsp salt

5 cloves garlic, minced

1 cup (60g) fresh cilantro leaves, coarsely chopped

1 hot red chili pepper, chopped

Juice of 1 large lemon

TO SERVE:

Lemon wedges

Toum (Garlic Sauce; page 248)

storage:

This dish is best served warm, but it can be stored in an airtight container in the refrigerator for 1 or 2 days.

notes:

Peel the potatoes or leave the skin on—it's your choice. Rinse them after chopping to remove any excess starch, and dry them well with a towel or in a salad spinner.

You can make this dish as a fresh salad instead by preparing the garlic, cilantro, chili pepper, and lemon juice and then tossing the mixture immediately into the roasted potatoes.

1. Cook the potatoes by deep-frying them, which is the traditional method, or baking or air-frying them. To deep-fry, heat the vegetable oil in a deep-fryer or large pan to 375°F (190°C). Salt the potatoes, and, working in batches to avoid overcrowding, cook for 5 or 6 minutes per batch or until light golden. Drain on a paper towel to remove excess oil, and repeat with remaining potatoes. To bake, spread the cubes on a baking sheet in a single layer, leaving some space between cubes so they can get golden and crispy. Drizzle with olive oil, toss, and bake in a preheated 400°F (200°C) oven for 30 to 35 minutes or until browned and tender, turning halfway through. To air-fry, cook the potatoes for 20 minutes at 350°F (180°C).

2. In a small skillet or a pan over medium heat, heat some olive oil. Add the garlic, and sauté for 2 minutes or until softened and fragrant.

3. Add the cilantro, and stir until just wilted. Add the chili pepper and lemon juice, and sauté for 1 more minute.

4. Toss together the potatoes and the cilantro mixture, and serve with lemon wedges and Toum.

Moutabal

EGGPLANT DIP

PREP TIME: **5 MINUTES**	COOK TIME: **20 MINUTES**	TOTAL TIME: **25 MINUTES**

SERVES: 4

VEGAN

GLUTEN FREE (omit pita)

This creamy eggplant dip is similar to baba ganoush, but with a few tweaks that make it smoky and delicious. It's easy to make, and it's even better the next day, so prepare it the day before you plan to serve it if you can. It's perfect for eating with pita bread and for mezze platters.

ingredients:

2 medium eggplants (about 550g)

1 tsp salt

2 cloves garlic, minced

2 tbsp **Tahini (Sesame Paste; page 250)**

3 tbsp freshly squeezed lemon juice

2 tbsp extra-virgin olive oil

1 tbsp chopped fresh flat-leaf parsley

2 tbsp pomegranate seeds

storage:

Store in an airtight container in the refrigerator for up to 5 days, or freeze for up to 3 months.

note:

If you don't have a gas stove, you can cook the eggplants in the oven. Preheat the broiler to low, place the eggplants on a baking sheet, and set as close to the heating element as possible. Broil for about 40 minutes, turning until the eggplants are charred on all sides.

1. Char each eggplant over a flame for about 5 minutes per side or until the entire skin is blackened and the eggplant is cooked. You can test if the eggplant is cooked by inserting a wooden skewer; it should go through easily.

2. To enhance their smoky flavor (and to make them simple to peel), immediately place the charred eggplants in a closed container or glass jar.

3. Let the eggplants cool slightly, until you can handle them comfortably, and then peel or scoop out the flesh into a bowl.

4. Mash the eggplant flesh using a fork. Add the salt, garlic, Tahini, and lemon juice, and mix well. Taste and adjust the seasonings as necessary.

5. Transfer the dip to a serving bowl. Top with olive oil, and sprinkle with parsley and pomegranate seeds. Enjoy with pita bread.

Sawdah

FRIED CHICKEN LIVER

PREP TIME: **10 MINUTES**	COOK TIME: **20 MINUTES**	TOTAL TIME: **30 MINUTES**

SERVES: 3
GLUTEN FREE

This protein-rich dish is a popular starter at Lebanese banquets. It's very sharp tasting and can be wrapped in sandwiches or eaten as is for breakfast. Lemon and Debs al Romman (Pomegranate Molasses; page 253) are good accompaniments for it.

1. Clean the livers, removing any sinewy bits, pat dry with a paper towel, and cut in half.

2. In a medium saucepan over high heat, heat the oil. Add the livers, and fry, turning a few times, for 12 to 15 minutes or until they become brown and have a firm texture.

3. Stir in the garlic, salt, pepper, and coriander. Cook, stirring, for 1 minute or until fragrant.

4. Add the lemon juice, and deglaze the pan. Add the Debs al Romman, and cook for 2 or 3 more minutes or until thickened.

5. Plate the livers over a bed of greens (if using). Sprinkle with sumac, pomegranate seeds, and parsley (if using), and serve with lemon wedges.

ingredients:

14 oz (400g) chicken livers

¼ cup (60ml) vegetable oil

2 cloves garlic, minced

1 tsp salt

½ tsp black pepper

½ tsp ground coriander

¼ cup (60ml) freshly squeezed lemon juice

¼ cup (44g) **Debs al Romman (Pomegranate Molasses; page 253)**

note:

You can substitute pomegranate juice for the lemon juice.

TO SERVE:

Arugula, flat-leaf parsley, or other leafy greens (optional)

1 tsp ground sumac (optional)

¼ cup (44g) pomegranate seeds (optional)

Chopped fresh flat-leaf parsley (optional)

Lemon wedges

storage:

Store the fried Sawdah in an airtight container in the refrigerator for up to 3 days, or freeze for up to 3 months.

Makanek

LEBANESE SAUSAGE

PREP TIME: **40 MINUTES** + 3 hours (chilling)	COOK TIME: **10 MINUTES**	TOTAL TIME: **50 MINUTES** + chilling

SERVES: 3
GLUTEN FREE

A type of Lebanese sausage, makanek are tasty and spicy without being hot. Serve them as a mezze or wrapped in a sandwich with fried potatoes, garlic, and pickles.

ingredients:

1 lb (450g) ground beef

1 tbsp pine nuts

½ tsp garlic powder

¼ tsp ground cloves

1 tsp cayenne

1 tsp black pepper

1½ tsp plus ½ cup (144g) salt, divided

1 tsp ground cardamom

1 tsp ground coriander

½ tsp ground cumin

1 tsp ground ginger

½ tsp ground nutmeg

½ tsp ground fenugreek

Sheep sausage casings

White vinegar (if casings are not precleaned)

4 tbsp vegetable oil

Juice of 1 medium lemon

TO SERVE:

Tomatoes

Pickles

Garlic paste

storage:

You can freeze the makanek for up to 2 months before they deteriorate in quality. If you plan on freezing them, do not cook them first.

note:

If you don't want to make sausages in the casings, you can mold the mixture into links. Fry or bake immediately, or, if you want to cook them later, arrange in a single layer on a tray, freeze for 4 hours, and then transfer to a freezer bag.

1. In a large mixing bowl, and using your hands, combine the beef, pine nuts, garlic powder, cloves, cayenne, pepper, 1½ teaspoons salt, cardamom, coriander, cumin, ginger, nutmeg, and fenugreek. Cover and refrigerate for 3 hours.

2. Meanwhile, prepare the casings. Sheep casings sold at your local butcher usually are cleaned and preserved with salt. If this is the case, soak them for at least 1 hour to loosen and remove all the salt. If the casings are not clean, soak them for 30 minutes in cool water, with ½ cup (144g) salt and 1 tablespoon white vinegar for each 1 cup (250ml) water. After soaking, rinse the inside and outside of each casing one at a time with fresh, cool water to remove any salt and vinegar residue. Knot one end of each casing, or tie it with a thread.

3. Fit a large piping bag with a ½-inch (1.25cm) round tip. Place some of the meat mixture in the piping bag; do not overfill. Pull the open end of the casing up over the tip of the piping bag, gathering it as much as possible. Gently stuff the casing with the meat filling, being careful not to split the casing. Every 4 to 6 inches (10–15cm), twist the casing a few times to form links. When you reach the end of the casing, tie another knot to finish it off. When ready to cook, cut through the twists to separate the links.

4. In a medium skillet over medium heat, heat the vegetable oil. Add the links, and cook, turning occasionally, for 10 minutes or until cooked through. Squeeze some lemon juice over the top, and stir.

5. Serve with tomatoes, pickles, and garlic paste. Or enjoy in pita bread as a sandwich.

Sujuk

SPICY LEBANESE SAUSAGE

PREP TIME: **40 MINUTES**
+ 3 hours (chilling)

COOK TIME: **10 MINUTES**

TOTAL TIME: **50 MINUTES**
+ chilling

SERVES: 3
GLUTEN FREE

Another Lebanese sausage, sujuk are similar to makanek, but whereas makanek are spicy but not hot, sujuk have a bit of heat. Sujuk are tasty served on their own or as a mezze.

ingredients:

1 lb (450g) ground beef
(80% lean/20% fat)

4 cloves garlic, minced

1 tbsp sweet paprika

1 tsp red chili powder

1 tsp black pepper

¼ tsp ground fenugreek

1½ tsp plus ½ cup (144g)
salt, divided

1 tsp ground cardamom

1 tsp ground coriander

½ tsp ground cumin

1 tsp ground ginger

½ tsp ground nutmeg

Sheep sausage casing

White vinegar (if
casings are not
precleaned)

½ cup (125ml) vegetable
oil

Juice of 1 medium lemon

TO SERVE:

Tomatoes

Lemon slices

Pickles

storage:

If you plan on freezing the
sujuk, do not add the garlic
with the other ingredients.

note:

Instead of all beef, you can
use 50 percent lean beef
and 50 percent lamb.

1. In a large mixing bowl, and using your hands, combine the beef, garlic, paprika, chili powder, pepper, fenugreek, 1½ teaspoons salt, cardamom, coriander, cumin, ginger, and nutmeg. Cover and refrigerate for 3 hours.

2. Meanwhile, prepare the casings. Sheep casings sold at your local butcher usually are cleaned and preserved with salt. If this is the case, soak them for at least 1 hour to loosen and remove all the salt. If the casings are not clean, soak them for 30 minutes in cool water, with ½ cup (144g) salt and 1 tablespoon white vinegar for each 1 cup (250ml) water. After soaking, rinse the inside and outside of each casing one at a time with fresh, cool water to remove any salt and vinegar residue. Knot one end of each casing, or tie it with a thread.

3. Fit a large piping bag with a ½-inch (1.25cm) round tip. Place some of the meat mixture in the piping bag; do not overfill. Pull the open end of the casing up over the tip of the piping bag, gathering it as much as possible. Gently stuff the casing with the meat filling, being careful not to split the casing. Every 6 to 10 inches (15–25.5cm), twist the casing a few times to form links. When you reach the end of the casing, tie another knot to finish it off. When ready to cook, cut through the twists to separate the links.

4. In a medium skillet over medium heat, heat the vegetable oil. Add the links, and cook, turning occasionally, for 10 minutes or until cooked through. Squeeze some lemon juice over the top, and stir.

5. Serve with tomatoes, lemon slices, and cucumber pickles. Or enjoy in pita bread as a sandwich.

Muhammara
ROASTED RED PEPPER DIP

PREP TIME: **10 MINUTES**	COOK TIME: **25 MINUTES**	TOTAL TIME: **35 MINUTES**

SERVES: 4
VEGAN
GLUTEN FREE (omit pita)

A popular dip, Muhammara has so many delicious flavor components—spicy, savory, sweet, smoky, nutty. It's often served as part of a mezze platter or as a side dish to grilled fish.

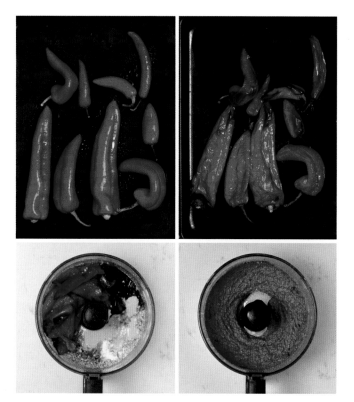

ingredients:

1 lb (450g) sweet red peppers

2.7 oz (78g) hot red chili peppers

2 cups (188g) raw walnuts

2 tbsp **Taratur (Tahini Sauce; page 251)**

2 tbsp **Debs al Romman (Pomegranate Molasses; page 253)**

½ tbsp salt

2 tbsp extra-virgin olive oil, plus more for serving

Pomegranate seeds

Chopped fresh flat-leaf parsley

½ tbsp smoked paprika (optional)

note:

Some versions of this recipe call for breadcrumbs as a thickener. I prefer it without, but if you want, you can add ½ cup (60g) before processing.

1. Preheat the oven to 350°F (180°C). Arrange all the peppers on a baking sheet, and roast for 20 to 25 minutes or until blistered and blackened. If you want to peel the skins, place the roasted peppers in a closed container or glass jar for a few minutes and then peel when cool enough to handle. Otherwise, set aside to let cool completely.

2. In a food processor, grind the walnuts until they're medium coarse. Set aside a few of the larger pieces for garnish.

3. Remove the stems from the peppers. To the walnuts in the food processor, add the roasted peppers, Taratur, Debs al Romman, salt, and olive oil. Process until smooth.

4. Transfer the muhammara to a serving plate. Drizzle with a bit of extra-virgin olive oil, and sprinkle some pomegranate seeds, parsley, and the reserved roughly chopped walnuts over top. Dust with paprika (if using), and serve. Enjoy with pita bread or chips.

Salatat Adas

LENTIL SALAD

PREP TIME: **10 MINUTES**	COOK TIME: **15 MINUTES**	TOTAL TIME: **25 MINUTES**

SERVES: 3

VEGAN

GLUTEN FREE

This super tasty lentil salad is nutritious and refreshing.
It can be served as a side or makes a hearty meal on its own.

ingredients:

1 cup (204g) dried green lentils, rinsed and any small stones discarded, or 2½ cups (188g) cooked

2–4 mini cucumbers (136g), chopped

3.5 oz (100g) cherry tomatoes, chopped

2 green onions (32g), chopped

¾ cup (45g) chopped fresh flat-leaf parsley

⅔ cup (20g) chopped fresh mint leaves

DRESSING:

¼ cup (60ml) extra-virgin olive oil

¼ cup (60ml) freshly squeezed lemon juice

3 large cloves garlic, minced

½ tsp ground cumin

1 tsp salt

½ tsp black pepper

note:

If you use dried lentils, be sure to look through them carefully after rinsing to find and discard any small stones that might have gotten in the package.

1. In a large pot over medium-high heat, bring the lentils and plenty of water to a boil. Simmer for 12 to 15 minutes or until al dente (not mushy).

2. In a small bowl, make the dressing. Mix together the olive oil, lemon juice, garlic, cumin, salt, and pepper.

3. In a large bowl, add the chopped cucumbers, tomatoes, and green onions. Add the cooked lentils, parsley, and mint. Pour the dressing over the top, mix to incorporate, and serve.

Salatat Hummus

CHICKPEA SALAD

PREP TIME: **10 MINUTES**	COOK TIME: **NONE**	TOTAL TIME: **10 MINUTES**

SERVES: 4

VEGAN

GLUTEN FREE

ingredients:

2 cups (454g) cooked chickpeas

3–4 medium tomatoes, chopped

1 long red chili pepper, chopped

2 small cucumbers (about 224g), chopped

3 green onions (47g), chopped

1 cup (60g) fresh flat-leaf parsley leaves

1 cup (25g) fresh mint leaves

2 cloves garlic, minced

1 tsp ground sumac

½ cup (125ml) extra-virgin olive oil

Zest and juice of 1 medium lemon

1 tsp salt

This nutritious chickpea salad is richly flavored and packed with protein and fresh vegetables. It's perfect for lunch or as a side dish.

1. In a large bowl, toss together all the ingredients.

2. Serve immediately, or chill until ready to serve.

storage:

Store in an airtight container in the refrigerator for up to 3 days.

Lebanese Salata

TOMATO CUCUMBER SALAD

| PREP TIME: **15 MINUTES** | COOK TIME: **NONE** | TOTAL TIME: **15 MINUTES** |

SERVES: 3

VEGAN

GLUTEN FREE

ingredients:

4 small cucumbers, diced

1 large tomato, diced

1 medium red chili pepper, diced

1 small red onion, diced

1 large clove garlic, minced

½ cup (125ml) extra-virgin olive oil

Juice of 1 medium lemon

½ tsp salt

½ tsp ground sumac

1 tbsp dried mint

Fresh mint leaves

note:

You can serve this immediately, but it's best if you refrigerate it for at least 1 hour before serving so the flavors can meld.

If you're craving a light and refreshing summer dish, this tomato cucumber salad is it. It's a perfect accompaniment to moujadara, moudardara, and kibbeh.

1. In a large bowl, add the cucumbers, tomato, chili pepper, onion, and garlic. Add the olive oil, lemon juice, salt, sumac, and dried mint, and toss to combine.

2. Garnish with fresh mint and serve immediately, or let chill so the flavors can develop.

Salatat al Raheb

MONK SALAD

PREP TIME: **10 MINUTES**	COOK TIME: **20 MINUTES**	TOTAL TIME: **30 MINUTES**

SERVES: 3

VEGAN

GLUTEN FREE

Monk salad is a refreshing and healthy dish that's usually part of a mezze. This simple and delicious salad combines fresh ingredients and smoked eggplant and makes a perfect side dish or weeknight dinner.

ingredients:

1 large eggplant (1 lb/450g)

Juice of 1 medium lemon

½ cup (37g) sliced green onion

½ cup (80g) pomegranate seeds, plus more for garnish

1½ cups (250g) chopped tomatoes

½ tsp salt

½ tsp black pepper

½ cup (30g) coarsely chopped fresh flat-leaf parsley leaves, plus more for garnish

1 tbsp **Debs al Romman (Pomegranate Molasses; page 253)**

2 tbsp extra-virgin olive oil

1. Char the eggplant over a flame for about 5 minutes per side or until the entire skin is blackened and the eggplant is cooked. You can test if the eggplant is cooked by inserting a wooden skewer; it should go through easily.

2. To enhance the smoky flavor (and to make it simple to peel), immediately place the charred eggplant in a closed container or glass jar.

3. Let the eggplant cool slightly, until you can handle it comfortably, and then peel or scoop out the flesh into a bowl.

4. Chop the eggplant roughly with a knife into medium pieces.

5. Add the remaining ingredients to the eggplant, and toss to combine.

6. Transfer to a serving bowl, and garnish with extra pomegranate seeds and parsley. Serve immediately or chill until ready to serve.

storage:

Store in an airtight container in the refrigerator for up to 3 days.

note:

If you don't have a gas stove, you can cook the eggplant in the oven. Preheat the broiler to low, place the eggplant on a baking sheet, and set as close to the heating element as possible. Broil for about 40 minutes, turning until the eggplant is charred on all sides.

Sambousek

CHEESE ROLLS

PREP TIME: **30 MINUTES** + 30 minutes (soaking) & 3 hours (freezing)	COOK TIME: **15 MINUTES**	TOTAL TIME: **45 MINUTES** + soaking & freezing

SERVES: 4

VEGAN (substitute vegan cheese)

Cheese rolls, also known as rakakat bi jebne in Lebanon, are a very popular appetizer, especially during Ramadan. They freeze beautifully so you can make them ahead and fry or bake them directly from the freezer.

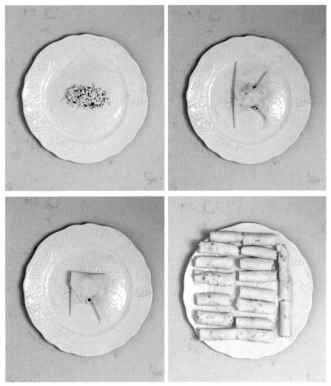

ingredients:

8 oz (225g) Akkawi or feta cheese

8 oz (225g) shredded mozzarella

1½ tbsp chopped fresh flat-leaf parsley

1 tbsp nigella seeds

18–20 spring roll wrappers

Vegetable oil, for frying

notes:

Freezing the rolls before frying them firms the cheeses so they don't get too melted as they cook.

If you'd prefer not to deep-fry the cheese rolls, you can bake them instead. Preheat the oven to 350°F (180°C). Spray the frozen cheese rolls with vegetable oil on all sides and evenly arrange on a baking sheet so they're not touching. Bake for 5 minutes per side.

You also can use an air fryer. Preheat it to 375°F (190°C). Cooking in batches as needed so you don't overcrowd the basket, arrange the rolls in an even layer so they're not touching. Air-fry for 2 minutes per side.

1. Shred the Akkawi, and soak the shreds in a bowl of cold water for 30 minutes to remove excess salt. If using feta instead of Akkawi, crumble the feta.

2. Drain the Akkawi. Add it to a mixing bowl with the mozzarella, parsley, and nigella seeds, and mix well.

3. Spread 1 tablespoon cheese mixture onto the center of each spring roll wrapper. To form a roll, fold two opposite corners of the wrapper to the middle over the cheese, bring the bottom corner over the middle, and roll up toward the top corner. Rub the last corner with a little water to secure the end and seal.

4. Arrange the rolls on a baking sheet so they're not touching, and freeze for 2 or 3 hours. Transfer the rolls to a freezer bag to store, or cook them from frozen.

5. Fill a heavy-bottomed pot about halfway with oil, set over medium-high heat, and heat to 350°F (180°C). Deep-fry the cheese rolls, a few at a time to avoid overcrowding the pot, for about 8 minutes or until they're golden.

6. Remove and drain on a paper towel. Serve warm.

Assoura

SEASONED DANDELION GREENS

PREP TIME: **5 MINUTES**	COOK TIME: **10 MINUTES**	TOTAL TIME: **15 MINUTES**

SERVES: 3
VEGAN
GLUTEN FREE

Also known as hindbeh, this dandelion green and onion dish is a very popular Lebanese mezze. It's also great in a sandwich.

ingredients:

1 lb (450g) dandelion greens, spinach, or a combination

1 tsp baking soda

⅔ cup (150ml) extra-virgin olive oil

2 medium yellow onions (225g), thinly sliced

½ tsp salt

1 medium lemon, cut into wedges

note:

The baking soda keeps the dandelion greens green and makes them cook faster.

1. In a large saucepan over high heat, bring the dandelion greens, baking soda, and water to cover to a boil. Cook for 5 minutes to fully wilt the greens.

2. Drain the water with a strainer, and press the dandelion greens to remove as much liquid as possible. When they're cool enough to handle, use your hands or a nut milk bag to squeeze out the rest of the water. Then either chop the leaves or leave them whole.

3. In the saucepan over medium-high heat, heat the oil. Add the onions, and fry for 5 minutes or until they're crispy and golden brown.

4. Lay the dandelion greens on a serving plate, season with salt, and top with the crispy onions and the oil used for frying the onions.

5. Serve with lemon wedges for drizzling. Enjoy with pita bread.

Salatet Laban

CUCUMBER YOGURT SALAD

PREP TIME: **5 MINUTES**	COOK TIME: **NONE**	TOTAL TIME: **5 MINUTES**

SERVES: 3

VEGAN (substitute almond or soy yogurt)

GLUTEN FREE

This refreshing and simple salad that's served cold is a welcome dish on hot days. It's also a wonderful side dish to mujadara and tomato bakleh.

56

ingredients:

2 cups (500ml) plain full-fat yogurt

1 clove garlic

½ tsp salt

1 tsp dried mint

5 mini cucumbers (about 340g), diced

Sprig of fresh mint

storage:

Store in an airtight container in the refrigerator for up to 2 or 3 days.

1. Add the yogurt to a medium bowl, and mince or grate the garlic directly into it. Add the salt and mint, and mix very well.

2. Stir in the cucumbers, garnish with fresh mint, and serve!

Shorbet Adas
RED LENTIL SOUP

PREP TIME: **5 MINUTES**	COOK TIME: **15 MINUTES**	TOTAL TIME: **20 MINUTES**

SERVES: 4

VEGAN (substitute vegetable stock or water)

GLUTEN FREE (omit pita)

This warm lentil soup is a staple during Ramadan dinners. It is comforting and filling and pairs perfectly with crunchy toast or pita chips.

ingredients:

- 1½ cups (315g) dried red lentils, rinsed and any small stones discarded
- 2 qt (2 liters) vegetable or chicken stock or water (see note)
- ¼ cup (60ml) extra-virgin olive oil
- 1 small yellow onion (90g), finely chopped
- ¼ cup (15g) finely chopped fresh flat-leaf parsley, plus more for garnish
- 1 tsp ground cumin
- 1 large lemon

notes:

If you're using water instead of vegetable or chicken stock, add ½ tablespoon salt or to taste.

Some people fry this with ghee, which makes it very tasty and rich, but I love the results when using olive oil.

1. Add the lentils and vegetable stock to a large pot, set over medium-high heat, and bring to a boil, uncovered. As the lentils boil, skim off the foam from the top. Reduce heat to low, cover, and simmer for 12 to 15 minutes or until very soft.

2. Meanwhile, in a medium pan over medium heat, heat the oil. Add the onion, and sauté for about 5 minutes or until the onion is softened.

3. Add the parsley, and sauté for 2 minutes.

4. Add the cooked lentils, remove from heat, and stir in the cumin. Garnish with parsley, and serve with a squeeze of lemon.

Warak Enab

STUFFED GRAPE LEAVES

PREP TIME: **45 MINUTES**	COOK TIME: **1 HOUR** + 30 minutes (cooling)	TOTAL TIME: **1 HOUR 45 MINUTES** + cooling

SERVES: 5

VEGAN

GLUTEN FREE

Full of fresh vegetables and herbs, these stuffed grape leaves are nutritious and delicious. Warak Enab is commonly served as part of a mezze for light summer meals or as an appetizer. You also can serve it warm as a main dish.

ingredients:

about 60 grape leaves (8 oz/250g)

2¼ cups (370g) small diced tomatoes

1 cup (100g) sliced green onions

1½ cups (90g) chopped fresh flat-leaf parsley

¾ cup (30g) chopped fresh mint

1 red chili pepper (17g), very finely chopped

2 cups (400g) short-grain rice, washed well, rinsed, and drained

1½ tbsp salt, divided

1 tsp black pepper

1 cup (250ml) extra-virgin olive oil, divided, plus more for greasing

3 medium tomatoes, sliced

3 medium russet potatoes, sliced

½ cup (125ml) freshly squeezed lemon juice

½ cup (125ml) water

2 medium lemons, cut into wedges

1. Wash the grape leaves individually in cold water, and remove the middle stem. If using fresh leaves, blanch them in boiling water for about 5 minutes or until soft and pale yellow-green. If using jarred brined leaves, skip the blanching but still rinse them well.

2. In a large bowl, combine the small diced tomatoes, onions, parsley, mint, red chili pepper, rice, half of the salt, the pepper, and ½ cup (125ml) olive oil.

3. To roll each leaf, place the textured side up on a cutting board or marble. Place 1 heaping tablespoon of the filling in the center of the leaf. Fold the sides over the filling, and tightly roll up the leaf from the bottom. Repeat with the remaining grape leaves until you're out of stuffing.

storage:

Store the cooked stuffed grape leaves in an airtight container in the refrigerator for up to 7 days.

note:

You can make the filling, stuff the grapes leaves, and store them before cooking them. Uncooked and stored in an airtight container, they'll keep for up to 4 days in the refrigerator or up to 3 months in the freezer.

4. Grease the bottom of a large stock pot or Dutch oven with olive oil. Add the sliced tomatoes in an even layer. Add the sliced potatoes in an even layer over the tomatoes. Neatly arrange the rolled grape leaves in rows over the potatoes, ensuring they don't touch the pot to avoid getting charred while cooking.

5. In a small bowl, combine the remaining ½ cup (125ml) olive oil, lemon juice, remaining salt, and water. Pour over the stuffed leaves. Invert a heat-safe plate on top of the grape leaves, and weight it down with something heat safe; I use a mortar.

6. Cook, uncovered, over medium-high heat for 15 minutes. Remove the weighted plate, cover the pot, reduce the heat to low, and cook for 45 minutes to 1 hour. Remove from the heat, uncover, and allow to sit for 30 minutes to cool and absorb any remaining liquids. (This helps prevent any leaves from unrolling.) You can check to see if the rolls are cooked by testing one from the top layer.

7. Transfer the tomatoes, potatoes, and grape leaves to a serving platter, and serve with lemon wedges.

Salatet Bakdounes

PARSLEY ONION SALAD

PREP TIME: **5 MINUTES**	COOK TIME: **NONE**	TOTAL TIME: **5 MINUTES**

SERVES: 3

VEGAN

GLUTEN FREE

ingredients:

1 cup (155g) white onion, thinly sliced

1 tbsp ground sumac

1 cup (60g) fresh flat-leaf parsley leaves

This parsley and onion salad is light and simple to prepare. It's often served as a condiment with grilled kafta, mashawi, and shawarma or as a garnish for sandwiches.

1. Place the sliced onions on a serving platter or in a bowl. Sprinkle the sumac over the top, and gently massage the onions with the spice.

2. Add the parsley, stir to combine, and serve.

Salatet Za'atar
OREGANO SALAD

PREP TIME: **5 MINUTES**	COOK TIME: **NONE**	TOTAL TIME: **5 MINUTES**

SERVES: 3

VEGAN

GLUTEN FREE

ingredients:

¾ cup (24g) fresh oregano leaves

2 medium red or white onions (53g), thinly sliced

½ tsp ground sumac

¼ tsp salt

Juice of ½ medium lemon

2 tbsp extra-virgin olive oil

note:

You only want the tender fresh oregano leaves for this salad, so remove and discard the stems.

This fresh, sour oregano salad is popular in southern Lebanon. It is perfect as a side salad with grilled meat and kafta (mashawi).

1. In a medium bowl, toss together all the ingredients, and serve.

Foul Moukalla

GREEN FAVA BEANS

PREP TIME: **5 MINUTES**	COOK TIME: **10 MINUTES**	TOTAL TIME: **15 MINUTES**

SERVES: 4

VEGAN

GLUTEN FREE

ingredients:

3 tbsp extra-virgin olive oil

2 cups (250g) fresh or frozen shelled fava beans

3 cloves garlic, minced

⅓ cup (20g) fresh cilantro leaves, chopped

1 tbsp thinly sliced small red chili pepper

1 tsp salt

¼ tsp black pepper

Lemon slices

This flavorful bean dish can be eaten as a side or a main. Serve it with pita bread as part of a traditional Lebanese mezze.

1. In a medium skillet over medium-low heat, heat the oil. Add the beans, and cook for 7 or 8 minutes, depending on the size of the beans, until they soften.

2. Add the garlic, cilantro, and chili pepper, and cook for a few more minutes. Season with salt and pepper, and remove from heat.

3. Serve with lemon slices. Enjoy with pita bread.

note:

Fava beans grow inside a thick pod. If using fresh beans, cut open the pod and remove the beans. Boil the beans in water for 2 minutes, transfer to iced water, cool for 5 minutes, and then squeeze each bean out of its outer white skin before using.

Loubieh bil Zeit

GREEN BEANS IN OLIVE OIL

PREP TIME: **5 MINUTES**	COOK TIME: **30 MINUTES**	TOTAL TIME: **35 MINUTES**

SERVES: 4

VEGAN

GLUTEN FREE

A popular dish in a traditional Lebanese mezze, these green beans are easy to make but surprisingly flavorful. Serve warm or cold as a side dish or a main.

ingredients:

¼ cup (60ml) extra-virgin olive oil

2 medium white onions, diced

4 cloves garlic, minced

1 lb (450g) fresh green beans, ends trimmed, and cut into 2-in (5cm) pieces

1 tsp salt

3 medium tomatoes (465g), diced

½ tsp black pepper

1 cup (250ml) water

storage:

Store in an airtight container in the refrigerator for up to 4 days.

1. In a medium pot over medium-high heat, heat the oil. Add the onions, and sauté for 5 minutes or until translucent and softened. Add the garlic, and sauté for 1 minute.

2. Add the green beans, sprinkle with salt, and sauté, stirring occasionally, for about 10 minutes or until the beans are wilted.

3. Stir in the tomatoes, pepper, and water. Cover and bring to a boil. Reduce heat to low, and simmer for 15 minutes or until tender.

4. Transfer to a serving plate. Serve warm or cold, and enjoy with pita bread.

Adas Bhamod

GREEN LENTIL SOUP

| PREP TIME: **15 MINUTES** | COOK TIME: **25 MINUTES** | TOTAL TIME: **40 MINUTES** |

SERVES: 5
VEGAN
GLUTEN FREE

A comforting warm soup on a cold day, Adas Bhamod
is loaded with green lentils and good-for-you vegetables.

ingredients:

1 russet potato (about 260g)

½ cup (125ml) vegetable oil

3 small yellow onions (375g), finely chopped

1 lb (450g) Swiss chard or spinach, stems and leaves chopped

2 cups (175g) carrots, cubed small

2 qt (2 liters) water, plus 1–2 cups (250–500ml) more as needed

2 cups (365g) dried green or brown lentils, rinsed and any small stones discarded

½ tsp black pepper

1 tbsp salt

1 tbsp ground cumin

Lemon or lime wedges

1. Peel and chop the potato into small cubes. Place the cubes in a bowl of water to prevent them from oxidizing.

2. In a large saucepan over medium heat, heat the oil. Add the onions, and sauté for 2 minutes. Add the chard and carrots, and sauté for 2 minutes or until the chard softens.

3. Add the water and lentils, and cook for 10 minutes.

4. Drain the potatoes, add them to the lentils, and cook, covered, for 10 minutes or until the potatoes are tender and the lentils are soft. Add more water, as needed, if the soup is too thick.

5. Add the pepper, salt, and cumin, and stir. Remove from the heat, and serve hot with lemon or lime wedges.

Mains

Lamb & Beef

Shawarma Lahmeh

BEEF SHAWARMA

PREP TIME: **10 MINUTES** + 4 hours (marinating)	COOK TIME: **15 MINUTES**	TOTAL TIME: **25 MINUTES** + marinating

SERVES: 5

VEGAN (substitute vegan meat alternative)

Filled with marinated and roasted meat and fresh and flavorful toppings, there's no wonder this sandwich is such a popular Lebanese street food.

ingredients:

2 lb (900g) beef steak cuts, thinly sliced

Pita bread

Hummus bi Tahini (Hummus; page 32)

Tomato, sliced

Fresh flat-leaf parsley leaves

Cucumber and turnip Kabis (Pickles; page 246)

Salatet Bakdounes (Parsley Onion Salad; page 63)

Tahini (Sesame Paste; page 250)

MARINADE:

1 large yellow onion, thinly sliced

4 cloves garlic, minced

1 medium lemon, thinly sliced

¼ cup (60ml) apple cider vinegar

1 cup (250ml) vegetable oil

1 tbsp salt

½ tsp black pepper

½ tsp ground coriander seeds

½ tsp ground bay leaves

2 tsp **Shawarma Spice (page 265)**

storage:

Store the marinated beef in an airtight container in the refrigerator for up to 3 days, or freeze for up to 3 months.

note:

The beef steak must be tender for this recipe. Filet mignon is a great choice, but you also can use sirloin or flap or flank steak.

1. In a large bowl, make the marinade. Combine the onion, garlic, lemon, vinegar, oil, salt, pepper, coriander, bay leaves, and Shawarma Spice.

2. Add the meat to the marinade, and mix thoroughly. Cover with plastic wrap or put in an airtight container, and marinate in the refrigerator for at least 4 hours or overnight.

3. Drain the beef from the marinade.

4. In a large skillet over medium-high heat, cook the beef for 15 to 20 minutes or until most of the juices have evaporated.

5. Serve in a pita bread sandwich: open a pita, and spread on some Hummus bi Tahini. Arrange the beef, sliced tomatoes, parsley, cucumber and turnip Kabis, and Salatet Bakdounes inside. Drizzle Tahini on top. Roll, and serve.

Mahashi

STUFFED VEGETABLES

PREP TIME: **1 HOUR**	COOK TIME: **1 HOUR**	TOTAL TIME: **2 HOURS**

SERVES: 5

VEGAN (substitute vegan meat alternative)

GLUTEN FREE

This recipe transforms humble zucchini and eggplant into delicious stuffed versions, filled with a flavorful seasoned beef mixture and swimming in a rich, tomato-based broth.

ingredients:

1¾ lb (800g) medium Lebanese zucchini

1 lb (500g) medium eggplants

20 fresh or jarred/ pickled grape leaves

9 small or medium tomatoes (1kg)

3 cups (750ml) vegetable broth or water

3 cloves garlic

1½ tsp dried mint

¼ cup (60ml) freshly squeezed lemon juice

STUFFING:

1 lb (450g) ground beef (80% lean/20% fat)

1 tbsp **Lebanese 7 Spices (page 261)**

1 tbsp black pepper

1 tbsp salt

2 cups (200g) short-grain rice, washed well, rinsed, and drained

2 tbsp vegetable oil

notes:

If you can't find Lebanese zucchini, you can substitute small regular zucchini.

And instead of ground beef, you can use ground lamb or vegan Soy Mince (page 224).

1. Cut the tops of the zucchini and eggplants, and hollow them out using a corer.

2. To make the stuffing, in a large bowl, combine the beef, Lebanese 7 Spices, pepper, salt, rice, and oil. Mix thoroughly.

3. Using a small spoon or your fingers, add some stuffing to each cored zucchini and eggplant. Don't stuff too tightly so the rice has room to expand as it cooks.

4. If using fresh grape leaves, blanch the leaves in a bowl of hot water for 3 minutes and then drain. If using jarred leaves, skip the blanching, but do rinse them well.

5. To roll each leaf, place the textured side up on a cutting board or marble. Place 1 heaping tablespoon (or a bit less so the rice can expand) of the stuffing in the center of the leaf. Fold the sides over the filling, and tightly roll up the leaf from the bottom. Repeat with the remaining grape leaves and stuffing.

6. Using kitchen twine, tie together 5 or 6 stuffed grape leaves into a neat parcel. Repeat with the remaining stuffed grape leaves.

note:

Instead of all tomato purée, you can use ¼ cup (239g) purée and 3 cups (750ml) water.

storage:

The stuffed vegetables are freezer friendly. They last for up to 3 months in an airtight container in the freezer.

7. In a food processor, blend the tomatoes to a smooth purée. You should have about 3 cups (750ml) purée. Transfer to a large, deep pot, and set over medium-high heat. Bring to a boil, and cook for about 15 minutes.

8. Add the vegetable broth or water, reduce the heat to medium, and simmer for 5 minutes.

9. Add the stuffed zucchini, eggplant, and grape leaves to the tomato mixture. Invert a heat-safe plate over the vegetables, and set a heat-safe bowl filled with water on top of the plate. This submerges the vegetables in the broth during cooking. Increase the heat to medium-high, and bring to a boil. Then reduce the heat to medium, and cook for about 30 to 40 minutes.

10. Remove the plate. Add the garlic, mint, and lemon juice, and simmer for 2 minutes.

11. Taste a stuffed zucchini for doneness; the rice inside should be cooked. If it's done, turn off the heat.

12. Serve the stuffed veggies hot, in a shallow bowl with some of the cooking liquid.

Hashwet al Kibbeh

KIBBEH STUFFING

PREP TIME: **5 MINUTES**	COOK TIME: **20 MINUTES**	TOTAL TIME: **25 MINUTES**

MAKES: 3 cups (500g)

VEGAN (substitute vegan meat alternative)

GLUTEN FREE

ingredients:

¼ cup (60ml) canola oil, divided

½ cup (70g) pine nuts

3 small yellow onions (250g), diced

1 lb (500g) minced lamb or beef

1 tbsp **Lebanese 7 Spices (page 261)**

1½ tsp salt

1 tsp black pepper

storage:

You can make a big batch of Hashwet al Kibbeh, divide it into portions, and freeze it in an airtight container for up to 3 months.

This kibbeh stuffing is a staple used in many Lebanese dishes (and several recipes in this chapter). It's easy to prepare and cooks quickly.

1. In a large skillet over medium heat, heat 2 tablespoons oil. Add the pine nuts, and sauté for 3 or 4 minutes or until golden brown. Immediately transfer the pine nuts to a plate, and set aside.

2. In the skillet, heat the remaining oil. Add the onions, and sauté for 5 minutes or until the onions are translucent.

3. Add the minced lamb, Lebanese 7 Spices, salt, and pepper. Stir and sauté for 10 minutes or until the meat is browned.

4. Add the toasted pine nuts, and stir to incorporate. The kibbeh stuffing is ready to use in recipes.

Kibbeh Maklieh

FRIED KIBBEH

PREP TIME: **30 MINUTES** + 30 minutes (soaking)	COOK TIME: **20 MINUTES**	TOTAL TIME: **50 MINUTES** + soaking

MAKES: 14–16 fried kibbeh balls

VEGAN (substitute vegan meat alternative)

Crispy and browned fried kibbeh balls are popular among the dishes at a Lebanese mezze meal. The aromatic flavors of Kamouneh spice in the crust makes Kibbeh Maklieh a hearty dish everyone will love.

ingredients:

3 cups (500g) fine **Bulgur Wheat** (Crushed Wheat; page 242)

4 cups (1 liter) water

1 cup (220g) **Kamouneh** (Green Bulgur Mix; page 257)

½ tbsp salt

1 lb (500g) lean ground beef (90% lean/10% fat, or fattier)

1 batch cooked **Hashwet al Kibbeh** (Kibbeh Stuffing; page 79)

Canola or vegetable oil, for deep-frying

notes:

If the casing mixture is soggy, add a bit of flour in step 2.

This recipe makes 12 fried kibbeh balls or enough kibbeh paste for 1 large Kibbeh bil Sanieh (Baked Kibbeh; page 86).

1. Soak the Bulgur Wheat in the water for at least 30 minutes.

2. In a large bowl, add the bulgur, Kamouneh, and salt. Then add the meat, and mix very well. Transfer to a food processor, and process to a smooth paste.

3. Sieve the Hashwet al Kibbeh to remove any excess liquid from the mixture, which could cause the balls to collapse.

4. Using your hands, roll about 2 teaspoons of the kibbeh paste into a ball. Make a hole in the center of the ball, and use your fingers to work the ball into a casing with thin walls. Stuff the casing with the Hashwet al Kibbeh and then carefully close the opening. Gently pull on two opposite ends of the casing to create the typical elongated shape of kibbeh balls.

5. Deep-fry the kibbeh in batches in 350°F (180°C) oil for about 5 minutes each or until the casing becomes dark brown. Using a slotted spoon, transfer the kibbeh to wire racks or paper towels to drain and cool.

6. Serve warm. Enjoy with Salatet Laban (Cucumber Yogurt Salad; page 56) or Lebanese Salata (Tomato Cucumber Salad; page 49).

Kibbeh bi Laban

KIBBEH IN YOGURT

| PREP TIME: **5 MINUTES** | COOK TIME: **20 MINUTES** | TOTAL TIME: **25 MINUTES** |

SERVES: 4

VEGAN (substitute vegan meat & yogurt alternatives)

Kibbeh bi Laban is a comforting blend of creamy, savory, and earthy. Once you have the prepared Kibbeh Maklieh (Fried Kibbeh; page 80), this recipe comes together quickly.

ingredients:

4 cups (1kg) plain full-fat yogurt

1 tsp salt

3 tbsp corn flour or cornstarch

12 **Kibbeh Maklieh (Fried Kibbeh; page 80)**

1 tbsp dried mint

3 cloves garlic (24g), minced

Toasted pine nuts

notes:

You can use frozen Kibbeh Maklieh in this recipe if you have some in the freezer. No need to thaw first before adding in step 2. If you're using frozen kibbeh balls that are not cooked or fried, cook them before adding in step 2. In a deep pan, heat some canola or vegetable oil to 350°F (180°C), and deep-fry the frozen kibbeh—do not thaw first—for 5 minutes each or until the casing becomes dark brown.

To toast the pine nuts, in a small dry (no oil) skillet over medium heat, toast the pine nuts, shaking the pan and stirring often, for about 3 minutes or until golden. Immediately transfer to a plate. Or you can fry them in 2 tablespoons oil over medium heat for 3 or 4 minutes or until golden brown.

1. In a small bowl, combine a bit of the yogurt with the salt and corn flour, and stir until no lumps remain. In a large pot, add the rest of the yogurt. Then add the yogurt and corn flour mixture, and stir. Alternatively, you can blend the yogurt, salt, and corn flour in a blender and transfer to the pot.

2. Add the Kibbeh Maklieh to the yogurt, and gently stir to coat.

3. Set the pot over medium heat, and cook, stirring constantly, for about 20 minutes.

4. Add the mint and garlic, stir, and remove from the heat.

5. Serve hot, topped with toasted pine nuts.

Sheikh el Mahshi

STUFFED EGGPLANT

PREP TIME: **30 MINUTES** + 30 minutes (sweating)	COOK TIME: **40 MINUTES**	TOTAL TIME: **1 HOUR 10 MINUTES** + sweating

SERVES: 6–8

VEGAN (substitute vegan meat alternative)

GLUTEN FREE (omit Riz bi Sh'arieh)

This is a cozy and satisfying dish at its best. These stuffed eggplants are simple and full of wonderful, rich flavor everyone will love.

ingredients:

3½ lb (1.5kg) baby eggplants

1 tsp salt

4 cups (1 liter) vegetable oil, for deep-frying

9 oz (250g) **Hashwet al Kibbeh (Kibbeh Stuffing; page 79)**

3½ cups (1kg) **Tomato Stew Sauce (page 230)**

Fresh oregano, chopped

Riz bi Sh'arieh (Rice with Vermicelli; page 241)

notes:

Salting the eggplants helps release, or "sweat," some of their liquid. It also makes the eggplants less likely to absorb the oil as they fry.

If you would like to bake the eggplants instead of frying, spray or brush them with vegetable oil, arrange on a baking sheet, and bake in a 350°F (180°C) oven for about 25 minutes.

If you can't find baby eggplants, small, long eggplants are a good alternative.

1. Make an incision on one side of each eggplant. On the opposite side, cut off (or peel off) some of the skin. Sprinkle salt over the eggplants, and place them in a strainer on top of a large bowl or on a cooling rack, and set aside for 30 minutes. Pat dry.

2. Preheat the oven to 350°F (180°C).

3. In a deep pan, heat the oil to about 330°F (170°C). Working in batches, fry as many eggplants as will fit in the pan for 4 minutes. Transfer to paper towels to drain, and carefully press gently with more paper towels to extract more oil.

4. To each cooled eggplant, add 1 or 2 tablespoons Hashwet al Kibbeh or until fully stuffed.

5. In a large, rimmed baking sheet or oven-safe dish, pour the Tomato Stew Sauce. Place the stuffed eggplants in the sauce, and bake for 15 to 20 minutes.

6. Garnish with oregano, and serve hot with Riz bi Sh'arieh.

Kibbeh bil Sanieh

BAKED KIBBEH

| PREP TIME: **30 MINUTES** | COOK TIME: **30 MINUTES** | TOTAL TIME: **1 HOUR** |

SERVES: 8–10

VEGAN (substitute vegan meat alternative)

This is the oven-baked alternative to kibbeh—and much quicker! It's a really healthy dish that's often served in Lebanese villages.

ingredients:

2 lb (1kg) casing paste from **Kibbeh Maklieh (Fried Kibbeh; page 80)**

15 oz (425g) **Hashwet al Kibbeh (Kibbeh Stuffing; page 79)**

32 pine nuts, soaked and drained

1–2 tbsp vegetable oil

note:

Soaking the pine nuts in water while you prepare the rest of the recipe prevents them from burning while the kibbeh bakes. Drain the pine nuts when ready to use.

1. Preheat the oven to 350ºF (180ºC).

2. Divide the Kibbeh Maklieh casing paste into equal halves.

3. Set half of the paste on a sheet of parchment paper, and roll out to a thin sheet large enough to fit your baking pan. (Shown is a 9-inch/23cm round pan.) Measure by setting the dish on the rolled paste and outlining it with a knife. Repeat with the remaining paste half.

4. Place one of the rolled halves in the bottom of the baking dish. Add the Hashwet al Kibbeh, and spread it to an even layer covering the whole bottom paste half. Add the second paste half on top, and carefully tuck in the edges.

5. Using a knife, make a long diagonal cut through the center and then make a second long cut perpendicular to the first. Cut each quarter into 2 for a total of 8 parts. Make a cut to separate each part into 2 and then another cut to separate them into 2 more for a total of 32 pieces.

6. Place 1 pine nut in each piece. Brush the top with oil.

7. Bake for 25 to 30 minutes. Serve hot.

Bamieh bil Lahme

OKRA & BEEF STEW

PREP TIME: **10 MINUTES**	COOK TIME: **40 MINUTES**	TOTAL TIME: **50 MINUTES**

SERVES: 5–6

VEGAN (substitute vegan meat alternative & vegetable stock)

GLUTEN FREE (omit Riz bi Sh'arieh)

If you love okra, this okra and beef stew will soon become a favorite. The cooked okra is moist and tender—and best of all, not slimy!—and the tomato sauce lends a hint of sweetness.

ingredients:

3 oz (83g) fresh cilantro

1½ lb (454g) fresh, frozen, or dried okra

Vegetable oil, for frying

3 tbsp olive oil

4 large cloves garlic (40g), finely chopped

1½ tbsp tomato paste

1½ cups (375ml) tomato juice

1 lb (450g) cooked beef or lamb shank (page 226)

2 cups (500ml) beef broth (page 226)

1½ tsp salt

½ tsp black pepper

1 tsp ground coriander seeds

¼ cup (60ml) freshly squeezed lemon juice

Riz bi Sh'arieh (Rice with Vermicelli; page 241)

Lemon wedges

notes:

If using dried okra, soak it in 2½ cups (625ml) hot water and ½ cup (125ml) white vinegar per every 1 cup (172g) dried okra for 2 hours. Drain and rinse.

This recipe calls for cooked beef or lamb and broth. I give instructions for braising the meat and producing a broth in the Braised Beef or Lamb & Broth recipe (page 226). This recipe's cook time does not include the 1½ hours required for cooking the meat and broth.

1. Separate the cilantro leaves from the stems. Finely chop the stems, and reserve the leaves.

2. If using fresh okra, wash and dry it completely, using a towel if needed. Cut off and discard the stems.

3. In a large, deep pan, heat about 2 inches (5cm) vegetable oil to 365°F (185°C). Add the okra, and fry 5 or 6 minutes. Transfer the okra to paper towels to drain.

4. In a large, deep pot over medium heat, heat the olive oil. Add the garlic and cilantro stems, and sauté for 30 seconds. Add the tomato paste, and sauté for 2 minutes.

5. Add the tomato juice, and simmer for 15 to 20 minutes or until reduced and thickened.

6. Add the cooked beef and broth, and mix well. Reduce the heat to low, and simmer for 20 minutes.

7. Add the okra, and cook, stirring occasionally, for 2 minutes. Add the salt, pepper, and coriander, and cook for 2 minutes.

8. Just before serving, add the lemon juice and cilantro leaves, stir, and serve hot with Riz bi Sh'arieh and lemon wedges.

Bazella w Riz

PEAS WITH RICE

PREP TIME: **10 MINUTES**	COOK TIME: **40 MINUTES**	TOTAL TIME: **50 MINUTES**

SERVES: 5

VEGAN (substitute vegan meat alternative & vegetable stock)

GLUTEN FREE (omit Riz bi Sh'arieh)

A hearty and filling traditional family meal, Bazella w Riz is rich in flavor and a great way to eat more good-for-you vegetables. Best of all, adults and kids alike will enjoy this nutritious stew.

ingredients:

3 oz (85g) fresh cilantro

3 tbsp olive oil

4 large cloves garlic (40g), finely chopped

1 tsp crushed coriander seeds

1½ tbsp tomato paste

1¾ cups (230g) diced carrots

1½ cups (375ml) tomato juice

1 lb (500g) cooked lamb or beef shank (page 226)

2 cups (500ml) beef broth (page 226)

3 cups (455g) fresh peas, washed and drained, or frozen

1½ tsp salt

½ tsp black pepper

¼ cup (60ml) freshly squeezed lemon juice

Riz bi Sh'arieh (Rice with Vermicelli; page 241)

Lemon wedges

storage:

Store in an airtight container in the refrigerator for up to 5 days, or freeze for up to 3 months.

notes:

For some heat, you can add a diced hot red chili pepper.

This recipe calls for cooked lamb or beef and broth. I give instructions for braising the meat and producing a broth in the Braised Beef or Lamb & Broth recipe (page 226). This recipe's cook time does not include the 1½ hours required for cooking the meat and broth.

1. Separate the cilantro leaves from the stems. Finely chop the stems. Reserve the leaves.

2. In a large deep pot over medium heat, heat the oil. Add the garlic, and sauté quickly for 30 seconds. Add the coriander, and stir.

3. Add the tomato paste, and sauté for 2 minutes. Add the carrots, and sauté for 2 minutes. Add the chopped cilantro stems, and stir.

4. Add the tomato juice, and simmer for 15 to 20 minutes or until reduced and thickened a bit.

5. Add the cooked lamb or beef and beef broth, and mix well. Reduce the heat to low, and simmer for 20 minutes.

6. Add the peas, and cook, stirring occasionally, for 2 minutes. Add salt and pepper, and cook for 2 minutes.

7. Just before serving, add the lemon juice and cilantro leaves, and stir.

8. Serve hot with Riz bi Sh'arieh and lemon wedges.

Fasolia w Riz

BUTTER BEAN STEW

PREP TIME: **10 MINUTES** + 6 hours (soaking)	COOK TIME: **45 MINUTES**	TOTAL TIME: **55 MINUTES** + soaking

SERVES: 4–5

VEGAN (substitute vegan meat alternative & vegetable stock)

GLUTEN FREE (omit Riz bi Sh'arieh)

Another warm and comforting stew along the lines of Bazella w Riz or Loubiah bi Lahmeh, Fasolia w Riz is a traditional meal full of flavor and rich in protein.

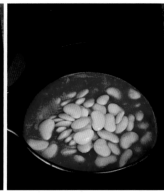

ingredients:

1 lb (500g) fresh or ⅔ lb (300g) dried white butter beans

4–6 cups (1–1.4 liters) water

2 tsp salt, divided

1 bay leaf

3 oz (85g) fresh cilantro

3 tbsp olive oil

4 large cloves garlic (40g), finely chopped

1½ tbsp tomato paste

1 tsp crushed coriander seeds

3 cups (750ml) tomato juice

1 lb (500g) cooked lamb or beef shank (page 226)

2 cups (500ml) beef broth (page 226)

½ tsp black pepper

¼ cup (60ml) freshly squeezed lemon juice

Riz bi Sh'arieh (Rice with Vermicelli; page 241)

Lemon wedges

storage:

Store in an airtight container in the refrigerator for up to 5 days, or freeze for up to 3 months.

note:

This recipe calls for cooked lamb or beef and broth. I give instructions for braising the meat and producing a broth in the Braised Beef or Lamb & Broth recipe (page 226). This recipe's cook time does not include the 1½ hours required for cooking the meat and broth.

1. If using fresh beans, rinse them well, drain, and add to a deep pot with 4 cups (1 liter) water. Bring to a boil over medium-high heat, skimming off any foam that rises to the top. Add ½ teaspoon salt and the bay leaf. Partially cover, and simmer for 10 minutes. When the beans are done, remove the bay leaf and then wash, drain, and set the beans aside. (If using dried beans, soak for at least 6 hours or overnight in cold water. Wash, drain, and continue as directed for the fresh beans except cook with 6 cups/1.4 liters water and simmer for 20 minutes.)

2. Separate the cilantro leaves from the stems. Finely chop the stems. Reserve the leaves.

3. In a large deep pot over medium heat, heat the oil, add the garlic, and sauté quickly for 30 seconds. Add the tomato paste, and stir. Add the coriander and chopped cilantro stems, and sauté for 2 minutes.

4. Add the tomato juice, and simmer for 15 to 20 minutes or until reduced and thickened a bit.

5. Add the cooked lamb or beef, beef broth, and cooked beans, and mix well. Reduce the heat to low, and simmer for 10 minutes.

6. Add the remaining 1½ teaspoons salt and pepper, and cook for 2 minutes.

7. Just before serving, add the lemon juice and cilantro leaves, and stir.

8. Serve hot with Riz bi Sh'arieh and lemon wedges.

Loubiah bi Lahmeh

GREEN BEAN STEW

PREP TIME: **10 MINUTES**	COOK TIME: **55 MINUTES**	TOTAL TIME: **1 HOUR 5 MINUTES**

SERVES: 4

VEGAN (substitute vegan meat alternative & vegetable broth)

GLUTEN FREE (omit Riz bi Sh'arieh)

If you're craving something warm, comforting, and filling for dinner, especially on a chilly day, try this green bean stew.

ingredients:

1⅔ lb (750g) fresh or frozen green beans

3 oz (85g) fresh cilantro

3 tbsp olive oil

4 large cloves garlic (40g), finely chopped

1½ tbsp tomato paste

1 tsp crushed coriander seeds

3 cups (750ml) tomato juice

2 cups (500ml) beef broth (page 226)

1 lb (500g) cooked beef shank (page 226)

1½ tsp salt

½ tsp black pepper

¼ cup (60ml) freshly squeezed lemon juice

Riz bi Sh'arieh (Rice with Vermicelli; page 241)

Lemon wedges

storage:

Store in an airtight container in the refrigerator for up to 5 days, or freeze for up to 3 months.

notes:

You can use trimmed, cut, and frozen green beans if fresh aren't in season.

This recipe calls for cooked beef and broth. I give instructions for braising the meat and producing a broth in the Braised Beef or Lamb & Broth recipe (page 226). This recipe's cook time does not include the 1½ hours required for cooking the meat and broth.

1. Rinse the fresh green beans, remove the stem ends, and cut the beans into medium pieces.

2. Separate the cilantro leaves from the stems. Finely chop the stems. Reserve the leaves.

3. In a large deep pot over medium heat, heat the oil. Add the garlic, and sauté quickly for 30 seconds. Add the tomato paste, and stir. Add the coriander, and sauté for 2 minutes. Add the chopped cilantro stems, and stir.

4. Add the green beans, and stir-fry for 5 minutes.

5. Add the tomato juice, and simmer for 10 to 15 minutes or until reduced and thickened a bit.

6. Add the beef broth, and bring to boil. Cover, reduce the heat to low, and simmer for 30 minutes.

7. Add the beef, season with salt and pepper, and cook for 2 minutes.

8. Just before serving, add the lemon juice and cilantro leaves, and stir.

9. Serve hot with Riz bi Sh'arieh and lemon wedges.

Fattet Hummus

CHICKPEAS IN YOGURT

PREP TIME: **5 MINUTES**	COOK TIME: **5 MINUTES**	TOTAL TIME: **10 MINUTES**

SERVES: 2

VEGAN (substitute vegan meat, butter, & yogurt alternatives)

No list of fattet recipes would be complete without a chickpea/hummus version. This Fattet Hummus is famous during Ramadan fast. It's a very filling and nutritious Iftar dish.

notes:

To make the crispy pita chips, cut 1 large or 2 small pitas into small squares and bake at 400°F (200°C) for 7 minutes or until golden and crispy.

This recipe calls for cooked lamb or beef. I give instructions for braising the meat in the Braised Beef or Lamb & Broth recipe (page 226). This recipe's cook time does not include the 1½ hours required for cooking the meat.

1. In a small saucepan over medium-low heat, fry the pine nuts in the ghee for 3 or 4 minutes or until they turn golden. Remove from the heat, and set aside.

2. In a medium bowl, combine the Tahini, yogurt, garlic, lemon juice, salt, and water (if using).

3. To assemble the fattet, in a large bowl, first place the pita chips on the bottom. Cover with the cooked chickpeas. Add the yogurt mixture and then the cooked meat.

4. Top with the toasted pine nuts and paprika, garnish with parsley, and serve immediately.

ingredients:

1½ tbsp pine nuts

2 tbsp ghee or melted butter

½ cup **Tahini (Sesame Paste; page 250)**

1½ cups (370g) plain full-fat yogurt

2 cloves garlic, minced

Juice of 1 small lemon

1 tsp salt

¼ cup (60ml) water to thin the sauce (optional)

1 cup (60g) crispy pita chips

2 cups (380g) cooked chickpeas or canned

1½ cups (315g) cooked beef or lamb shank (page 226)

¼ tsp sweet paprika

Sprig of fresh flat-leaf parsley

Laban Immo

BRAISED LAMB WITH YOGURT

PREP TIME: **5 MINUTES**	COOK TIME: **25 MINUTES**	TOTAL TIME: **30 MINUTES**

SERVES: 5

VEGAN (substitute vegan meat & yogurt alternatives)

GLUTEN FREE

Low-carb Laban Immo is a quick, easy, and refreshing meal. It's great for a light bite on hot summer nights.

1. In a medium pot over high heat, combine the rice, water, and olive oil. Bring to a boil, cover, reduce the heat to medium-low, and simmer for 15 minutes.

2. Meanwhile, in a large pot, add the yogurt, corn flour, and salt. Using a handheld blender, blend well. Set the pot over medium-high heat, and bring the contents to a boil, stirring continuously. Reduce the heat to medium-low.

3. Add the cooked meat to the yogurt mixture, along with the broth. Simmer, stirring constantly, for 10 minutes.

4. In a small saucepan over medium-low heat, fry the pine nuts in the butter for 3 or 4 minutes or until they turn golden. Remove from the heat.

5. Remove the cooked rice from the heat, and let sit, covered, for 10 minutes. Fluff the rice with a fork.

6. Transfer the meat and yogurt mixture to a serving dish, garnish with pine nuts, and serve hot with rice.

ingredients:

1 cup (200g) short-grain rice, washed well, rinsed, and drained

1¼ cups (310ml) water

1 tsp olive oil

8 cups (2kg) plain full-fat yogurt

½ cup (120g) corn flour

1 tbsp salt

2 lb (1kg) cooked mawzat lamb or beef (page 226)

2 cups (500ml) lamb or beef broth (page 226)

¾ cup (100g) pine nuts

1 tbsp butter

note:

This recipe calls for cooked lamb or beef and broth. I give instructions for braising the meat and producing a broth in the Braised Beef or Lamb & Broth recipe (page 226). This recipe's cook time does not include the 1½ hours required for cooking the meat and broth.

Sabanekh w Riz

SPINACH WITH RICE

PREP TIME: **5 MINUTES**	COOK TIME: **25 MINUTES**	TOTAL TIME: **30 MINUTES**

SERVES: 3–4

VEGAN (substitute vegan meat alternative)

GLUTEN FREE (omit Riz bi Sh'arieh)

Sabanekh w Riz is a warm, hearty, healthy spinach dish. It's an especially easy dinner recipe when you don't have a lot of time—or energy—to cook.

ingredients:

13½ cups (800g) fresh or frozen spinach

1½ cups (165g) fresh cilantro

4 tbsp vegetable oil, divided

6 small cloves garlic, minced

10 oz (265g) lean ground beef (or minced lean meat)

1 tsp salt

¼ tsp black pepper

½ tsp **Lebanese 7 Spices (page 261)**

3 tbsp pine nuts

¼ cup (60ml) freshly squeezed lemon juice

Riz bi Sh'arieh (Rice with Vermicelli; page 241)

1. If using fresh spinach, wash well, chop (I include the stems, too), and set aside.

2. Separate the cilantro leaves from the stems. Chop the stems. Reserve the leaves.

3. In a large pot over medium heat, heat 3 tablespoons oil. Add the garlic and cilantro stems, and sauté quickly for 30 seconds.

4. Add the beef, salt, pepper, and Lebanese 7 Spices, and fry for 6 or 7 minutes or until cooked.

5. Add the chopped spinach in batches, letting each batch wilt before adding the next. (It wilts quickly.) After about 5 minutes, when the spinach is almost cooked, add the chopped cilantro leaves, and cook for 2 more minutes.

6. Toast the pine nuts in a small pan over medium-low heat with the remaining 1 tablespoon oil for 3 or 4 minutes or until they turn golden.

7. Serve hot, topped with the toasted pine nuts and lemon juice, and with Riz bi Sh'arieh.

Malfouf Mehshi
STUFFED CABBAGE

PREP TIME: **30 MINUTES**	COOK TIME: **1 HOUR**	TOTAL TIME: **1 HOUR 30 MINUTES**

SERVES: 6

VEGAN (substitute vegan meat alternative)

GLUTEN FREE

These classic beef-and-rice-stuffed cabbage rolls are always a hit. They're light and healthy, yet comforting.

ingredients:

3½ lb (1.5kg) head cabbage, washed and cored

2 heads garlic, cloves separated

1 tbsp dried mint

¼ cup (60ml) freshly squeezed lemon juice

2 tbsp vegetable oil

Lemon wedges

2 tbsp **Debs al Romman (Pomegranate Molasses; page 253)** (optional)

STUFFING:

1 lb (500g) lean ground beef (80% lean/20% fat) or ground lamb

1 tbsp **Lebanese 7 Spices (page 261)**

1 tbsp salt

1 tbsp black pepper

2 cups (400g) short-grain rice, washed well, rinsed, and drained

2 tbsp vegetable oil

1. In a large pot over high heat, bring enough water to cover the cabbage to a boil. Plunge the cabbage in the boiling water for 2 or 3 minutes to blanch. Remove the cabbage and allow to cool. Without tearing them, trim off the whole outer leaves as they get soft and flexible. Set aside, and repeat as needed for the inner leaves.

2. To prepare the stuffing, in a large bowl, combine the beef, Lebanese 7 Spices, salt, pepper, rice, and 2 tablespoons oil.

3. Lay a cabbage leaf on a cutting board. Remove and reserve the hard rib from the base of the leaf, and cut the leaf to the size you prefer. Spread about 1 tablespoon stuffing in the middle of the leaf, leaving a little space on both edges, and roll the leaf around the filling, closing the edges as you roll. Repeat with the remaining stuffing and leaves.

variation:

Instead of ground beef, you can substitute ground lamb or vegan Soy Mince (page 224).

4. In the bottom of the large pot, place the reserved ribs, some garlic cloves, and a layer of unrolled cabbage leaves. Add the cabbage rolls, side by side in rows over the first layer, with more garlic between to taste. Add water just to cover the rolls. Invert a heat-safe plate on top of the rolls, and weight it down with something heat safe.

5. Set over medium-high heat, and bring to a boil. Reduce the heat to medium-low, and cook for about 45 minutes or until the rice is cooked inside the cabbage roll in the top layer and most of the water has evaporated.

6. Add the mint, lemon juice, and remaining 2 tablespoons oil, cover, and simmer for 10 minutes.

7. Serve hot with lemon wedges and a drizzle of Debs al Romman (if using).

Mahshi Ardi Shawki

STUFFED ARTICHOKES

PREP TIME: **10 MINUTES**   COOK TIME: **40 MINUTES**   TOTAL TIME: **50 MINUTES**

SERVES: 5–6

VEGAN (substitute vegan meat alternative)

GLUTEN FREE (omit Riz bi Sh'arieh)

ingredients:

1½ lb (715g) frozen, fresh, or canned artichoke bottoms

2 tbsp canola or vegetable oil

3½ cups (1kg) **Tomato Stew Sauce (page 230)**

9 oz (250g) **Hashwet al Kibbeh (Kibbeh Stuffing; page 79)**

Fresh flat-leaf parsley, chopped

Riz bi Sh'arieh (Rice with Vermicelli; page 241)

note:

In step 2, instead of baking the artichokes, you can deep-fry them in 355°F (180°C) oil for 3 minutes. Drain on paper towels before filling.

These tender stuffed artichokes are easy to prepare if you use canned or frozen artichoke bottoms. The tomato sauce adds a pop of bright flavor, and the rice rounds out this hearty dish.

1. Preheat the oven to 350°F (180°C).

2. Spray or brush the artichokes with some oil. Arrange the artichokes on a baking sheet, and bake for about 20 minutes.

3. In a large, oven-safe skillet or baking dish, pour the Tomato Stew Sauce. Arrange the baked artichokes in the sauce, and fill them with the Hashwet al Kibbeh.

4. Bake again for 15 to 20 minutes.

5. Garnish with parsley, and serve hot with Riz bi Sh'arieh.

Batata Soufflé
MASHED POTATO SOUFFLÉ

| PREP TIME: **10 MINUTES** | COOK TIME: **1 HOUR 10 MINUTES** | TOTAL TIME: **1 HOUR 20 MINUTES** |

SERVES: 9

VEGAN (with vegan meat, milk, & butter alternatives)

Cold days turn warm with this earthy-flavored dish you can make with just a few ingredients. It's spiced with my favorite Kamouneh mix (in the kibbeh stuffing) and tastes amazing.

ingredients:

4 lb (2kg) russet or Yukon Gold potatoes, washed well

4 tbsp butter

½ cup (125ml) milk

1 tbsp salt

¼ tsp ground nutmeg

1 tbsp olive oil

3 cups (500g) **Hashwet al Kibbeh (Kibbeh Stuffing; page 79)**

2 cups (100g) breadcrumbs or minced kaak

storage:

Store in an airtight container in the refrigerator for up to 3 to 5 days, or freeze for up to 2 months.

1. Place the potatoes in a medium pot, and add water to cover plus a couple inches more. Set over medium heat, and cook for about 50 minutes until the potatoes are fully cooked and soft.

2. Drain the potatoes, peel, and mash them in a bowl using a potato masher or ricer.

3. Add the butter, milk, salt, and nutmeg to the potatoes, and mix well.

4. Preheat the oven to 355°F (180°C). Brush the olive oil in the bottom of a 9×9-inch (23×23cm) baking pan.

5. Add half of the mashed potatoes to the prepared baking pan, and spread into an even layer. Top the potatoes with the Hashwet al Kibbeh, and spread into an even layer. Add the other half of the mashed potatoes on top of the kibbeh, and gently spread to an even layer.

6. Cover the top potato layer with breadcrumbs, and bake for 20 minutes or until the top is golden.

7. Allow to cool before cutting into squares and serving.

Ablama

STUFFED ZUCCHINI IN YOGURT SAUCE

PREP TIME: **10 MINUTES**	COOK TIME: **45 MINUTES**	TOTAL TIME: **55 MINUTES**

SERVES: 4

VEGAN (substitute vegan meat & yogurt alternatives)

GLUTEN FREE

Ablama is fresh zucchini stuffed with a hearty meat filling and topped with a yogurt sauce. It's fresh, creamy, and delectable.

ingredients:

2 lb (1kg) small zucchini, washed, tops cut off, and hollowed out using a corer

9 oz (250g) **Hashwet al Kibbeh (Kibbeh Stuffing; page 79)**

2 tbsp plus 1 tsp olive oil, divided

4 cups (1kg) plain full-fat yogurt

3¼ cups (810ml) water, divided

1 tbsp salt

3 tbsp corn flour

1 cup (200g) short-grain rice, washed well, rinsed, and drained

1¾ tbsp pine nuts

2 cloves garlic (16g), minced

1 tsp dried mint

1. Preheat the oven to 400°F (200°C). Fill the zucchinis with the Hashwet al Kibbeh, set in a baking pan, and brush with 1 tablespoon oil. Bake for 25 to 30 minutes or until the skin turns golden brown.

2. In a food processor, blend the yogurt, 2 cups (500ml) water, salt, and corn flour. Transfer to a large pot, set over medium heat, and cook, stirring constantly, for 15 minutes or until the yogurt begins to boil and thickens.

3. In a medium pot over high heat, combine the rice, remaining 1¼ cups (310ml) water, and 1 teaspoon oil. Bring to a boil, cover, reduce the heat to medium-low, and simmer for 15 minutes. Remove from the heat, and let sit, covered, for 10 minutes. Fluff with a fork before serving.

4. In a small saucepan over medium-low heat, toast the pine nuts with the remaining 1 tablespoon oil for 3 or 4 minutes or until they turn golden. Remove from the pan, and set aside.

5. In the same oil, fry the garlic and mint, and add to the yogurt mixture.

6. Pour the yogurt mixture over the cooked zucchini, garnish with toasted pine nuts, and serve hot with rice.

Shish Barak

LEBANESE DUMPLINGS IN YOGURT SAUCE

PREP TIME: **30 MINUTES** + 30 minutes (resting)	COOK TIME: **30 MINUTES**	TOTAL TIME: **1 HOUR** + resting

SERVES: 4

VEGAN (substitute vegan meat, yogurt, & butter alternatives)

Shish Barak, tender dumplings in a creamy yogurt sauce, is luscious yet light. It's a family-approved dish you'll all look forward to.

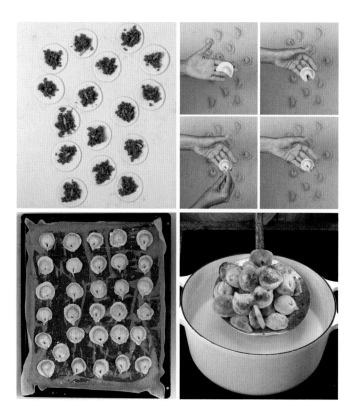

1. To make the dumpling dough, in a large bowl, mix the flour and ¼ teaspoon salt. Gradually add water, and knead until a soft dough forms. Cover with plastic wrap, and set aside for 30 minutes.

2. Preheat the oven to 355°F (180°C). Line a baking sheet with parchment paper.

3. Roll out the rested dough to ¼-inch (0.5cm) thick, and cut out 30 to 35, 2-inch (5cm) circles. Place 1 teaspoon Hashwet al Kibbeh in the center of each circle. Fold the circle in half, press the edges together, and bring the corners together. Set on the baking sheet, and bake for 10 minutes. Remove from the oven.

4. For the yogurt sauce, in a food processor, blend the yogurt, corn flour, and 1½ teaspoons salt. Transfer to a large pot, set over medium heat, and bring to a boil, stirring. Reduce the heat to low, add the dumplings, and simmer, stirring constantly, for 10 minutes.

5. In a small skillet, toast the pine nuts in the butter for 3 or 4 minutes or until golden. Set aside. Add the garlic and cilantro to the skillet, and stir-fry for 1 minute.

6. Garnish the dumplings and yogurt sauce with the pine nuts, garlic, and cilantro, and serve hot.

ingredients:

2 tbsp pine nuts

2 tbsp butter

6 cloves garlic (25g)

2 tbsp fresh cilantro, chopped

DUMPLINGS:

1½ cups (220g) all-purpose flour

¼ tsp salt

½ cup (125ml) water

7 oz (200g) **Hashwet al Kibbeh (Kibbeh Stuffing; page 79)**

YOGURT SAUCE:

4 cups (1kg) plain full-fat yogurt

3 tbsp corn flour

1½ tsp salt

Kibbeh Nayyeh
RAW BEEF

PREP TIME: **20 MINUTES** + 30 minutes (freezing)	COOK TIME: **NONE**	TOTAL TIME: **20 MINUTES** + freezing

SERVES: 3

Kibbeh Nayyeh, raw minced beef flavored with earthy spices, is a popular dish served as a main or mezze during traditional Lebanese dinners. The raw meat must be fresh. Purchase it from a trusted butcher the same day you're preparing it.

ingredients:

¼ cup (40g) fine **Bulgur Wheat (Crushed Wheat; page 242)**

¼ cup (60ml) cold water

4.5 oz (120g) fresh veal meat and liyyeh or lean lamb (for 4 oz/ 116g malseh)

⅓ cup (40g) **Kamouneh (Green Bulgur Mix; page 257)**

2 tbsp extra-virgin olive oil, plus more for serving

¼ tsp salt

note:

The meat must be cold, it must be fresh, and it must be cut on the same day you're going to eat it.

1. Soak the Bulgur Wheat in the cold water for 5 minutes.

2. To prepare the fresh meat, cut it into cubes (if you're going to use a food processor in step 3) or wide strips (if you're going to use the traditional method in step 3), and freeze for 30 minutes before beating it. This firms the meat so it can be ground much more easily, and it stays cold while you're working with it.

3. In a food processor, grind the frozen meat for several minutes until a fine pasty texture is achieved and the meat forms a ball in the food processor bowl. Alternatively, and the traditional method used especially in rural areas, you can beat it by hand. This is usually done by knocking the meat thoroughly using a special wooden hammer on a kibbeh mortar, or special stone. My ancestors insisted on doing it this way to get the highest-quality malseh. If some white ligaments or nerves appear in the meat, remove them to get a perfectly smooth and lean malseh.

4. Using your hands, form the malseh into a large ball, and place in a bowl. Add the soaked bulgur, Kamouneh, olive oil, and salt.

storage:

Kibbeh Nayeh must be eaten as soon as it's prepared; otherwise, it's not safe.

Any leftover kibbeh can be made into kibbeh balls stuffed with kibbeh meal or transformed into flat patties and frozen. If properly stored, it can last and maintain good quality for up to 3 months.

note:

It bears repeating: you must keep the fresh meat cold until you're ready to prepare it.

5. Use clean hands to combine and knead the mixture until it's well mixed.

6. Transfer the mixture to a plate, spread in an even layer, and use a fork to make pretty patterns or indents to hold the oil.

7. Serve immediately with more extra-virgin olive oil. Enjoy with radishes, cucumbers, green onions, or any fresh vegetables.

Frakeh

RAW BEEF

PREP TIME: **15 MINUTES** + 30 minutes (freezing)	COOK TIME: **NONE**	TOTAL TIME: **15 MINUTES** + freezing

SERVES: 4

ingredients:

5 oz (140g) fresh veal meat and liyyeh
or lean lamb (for 5 oz/136g malseh)

½ cup (78g) fine **Bulgur Wheat
(Crushed Wheat; page 242)**

⅓ cup (40g) **Kamouneh (Green Bulgur
Mix; page 257)**

2 tbsp extra-virgin olive oil

¼ tsp salt

storage:

Frakeh must be eaten as soon as it's
prepared; otherwise, the bulgur is not
crisp and the meat is not safe. Any frakeh
leftovers can be made into kibbeh by
adding little water, kneading, forming into
balls, and freezing in an airtight container
for up to 3 months.

note:

You must keep the fresh meat cold until
you are ready to prepare it.

Frakeh is similar to Kibbeh Nayeh (Raw Beef; page 112), but it's shaped
by hand rather than into a mound. The first few preparation steps are
the same as for Kibbeh Nayeh, except this Bulgur Wheat is not soaked
and this mixture is formed into patties.

1. Follow steps 2, 3, 4, and 5 of the Kibbeh Nayeh recipe. (Skip step 1;
   don't soak the Bulgur Wheat before adding it in step 4 with the
   Kamouneh, olive oil, and salt.)

2. Shape the mixture into small balls, and use your fingers to make
   a rippled shape by squeezing the balls softly.

3. Serve immediately on a plate around the extra Kamouneh, and enjoy
   with extra-virgin olive oil, radishes, tomatoes, green onions, or any
   fresh vegetables.

Kafta Nayyeh

LEBANESE RAW BEEF MIX

PREP TIME: **5 MINUTES**	COOK TIME: **NONE**	TOTAL TIME: **5 MINUTES**

MAKES: 1.37 pounds (624g)

GLUTEN FREE

ingredients:

1 lb (½kg) minced beef (80% lean/ 20% fat) or lamb

2 small yellow onions (119g), finely chopped

½ cup (30g) fresh flat-leaf parsley, finely chopped

2 tsp salt

1 tsp black pepper

1 tsp **Lebanese 7 Spices (page 261)**

Kafta Nayyeh is mostly grilled in the summer as a quick lunch or used in other recipes like Dawood Basha (Meatball Stew; page 120) or Kafta bil Sanieh (Kofta & Potatoes; page 118).

1. In a large bowl, combine the beef or lamb, onions, parsley, salt, pepper, and Lebanese 7 Spices until all the ingredients are incorporated.

2. Use the mix immediately in relevant recipes.

Arayes Kafta

KAFTA NAYYEH WITH PITA BREAD

PREP TIME: **5 MINUTES**	COOK TIME: **5 MINUTES**	TOTAL TIME: **10 MINUTES**

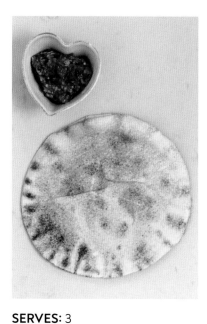

SERVES: 3

ingredients:

Kafta Nayyeh (Lebanese Raw Beef Mix; page 116)

3 pita bread

Also known as kallag, Arayes Kafta is part of a meal served in Lebanese restaurants with mashawi. It's easy, quick, and perfect for a weeknight meal.

1. Preheat a charcoal grill or the oven to 325°F (170°C).

2. Spread the Kafta Nayyeh on the pita bread in a thin layer.

3. Grill directly on the grate or rack for about 2 minutes per side.

4. Serve hot. Enjoy with chili paste spread.

Kafta bil Sanieh

KAFTA NAYYEH & POTATOES

| PREP TIME: **15 MINUTES** | COOK TIME: **1 HOUR 5 MINUTES** | TOTAL TIME: **1 HOUR 20 MINUTES** |

SERVES: 6
GLUTEN FREE (omit Riz bi Sh'arieh)

Flavorful, juicy Kafta Nayyeh is combined with potatoes, fresh tomatoes, and a fabulous homemade tomato sauce to form a perfect one-pan comfort meal. It's also delicious with Riz bi Sh'arieh (Rice with Vermicelli; page 241).

ingredients:

1½ lb (590g) russet potatoes

Kafta Nayyeh (Lebanese Raw Beef Mix; page 116)

3 cups (900g) **Tomato Stew Sauce (page 230)**

3 small yellow onions (206g), sliced into rounds

6 small tomatoes (392g), sliced into rounds

Fresh flat-leaf parsley

note:

To prevent the potato rounds from turning brown while the Kafta Nayyeh patties bake, you can submerge them in water and then drain well just before using.

1. Preheat the oven to 355°F (180°C).

2. Peel the potatoes, and slice into equal rounds. Wash well, and drain.

3. Shape the Kafta Nayyeh into patties about the same size as the potato, onion, and tomato rounds, and place them on a baking sheet. Bake for about 20 minutes.

4. Pour the Tomato Stew Sauce over and around the cooked Kafta Nayyeh patties.

5. Layer the potato, onion, and tomato rounds over the cooked Kafta Nayyeh patties. Cover the pan with foil, and bake for 45 minutes or until the potatoes are soft and easily pierced with a fork.

6. Garnish with parsley, and serve hot. Enjoy with Riz bi Sh'arieh (Rice with Vermicelli; page 241).

Dawood Basha

MEATBALL STEW

PREP TIME: **15 MINUTES**	COOK TIME: **35 MINUTES**	TOTAL TIME: **50 MINUTES**

SERVES: 4

GLUTEN FREE (omit Riz bi Sh'arieh)

This meatball stew is rich, hearty, and satisfying. It's similar to Kafta bil Sanieh, but with a tomatoey twist that will delight and comfort the whole family.

ingredients:

22 oz (624g) freshly prepared **Kafta Nayyeh
(Lebanese Raw Beef Mix; page 116)**

Cooking oil spray

3½ cups (1kg) **Tomato Stew Sauce (page 230)**

Fresh flat-leaf parsley

Riz bi Sh'arieh (Rice with Vermicelli; page 241)

note:

For safety, it's important that you work with freshly
prepared Kafta Nayyeh mixture, or freshly prepared
and then immediately frozen.

1. Preheat the oven to 355°F (180°C).

2. Using your hands, form the freshly prepared
   Kafta Nayyeh mixture into meatball-size balls
   about 1.34 ounces (38g) each. You should have
   about 15 balls.

3. Place the balls on a baking sheet, lightly coat
   with cooking oil spray, and bake for 20 minutes
   or until brown on all sides.

4. In a large skillet over medium-high heat, warm the
   Tomato Stew Sauce. Add the baked Kafta Nayyeh
   balls to the stew, and simmer for 15 minutes.

5. Garnish with parsley, and serve hot with Riz bi
   Sh'arieh.

Fawaregh

STUFFED SAUSAGE

PREP TIME: **35 MINUTES**	COOK TIME: **1 HOUR**	TOTAL TIME: **1 HOUR 35 MINUTES**
+ 30 minutes (soaking)		+ soaking

SERVES: 4

GLUTEN FREE

Fawaregh, seasoned meat and rice stuffed sausages, are rich and flavorful. They're sure to be a hit with sausage lovers.

ingredients:

Clean sheep or lamb sausage casings

3 tsp salt, divided

White vinegar

1 cup (200g) short-grain rice, washed well, rinsed, and drained

1 lb (500g) minced lamb or beef

½ tsp black pepper

½ tsp ground cinnamon

¼ tsp ground allspice

11 pearl onions

2 bay leaves

5–6 cardamom pods

5 whole cloves

1 tsp black peppercorns

storage:

Store any leftovers in an airtight container in the refrigerator for up to 2 days.

1. Prepare the casings. Sheep casings sold at your local butcher usually are cleaned and preserved with salt. If this is the case, soak them for at least 1 hour in a bowl of water to loosen and remove all the salt. (If the casings are not clean, soak them for 30 minutes in cool water, with 1 teaspoon salt and 1 tablespoon white vinegar for each 1 cup water.) After soaking, rinse the inside and outside of each casing one at a time with fresh, cool water to remove any salt and vinegar residue. Knot one end of each casing or tie it with a thread.

2. Place the rice in a large bowl. Add the meat, 1 teaspoon salt, pepper, cinnamon, and allspice, and mix well.

3. Fit a large piping bag with a ½-inch (1.25cm) round tip. Place the rice and meat mixture in the piping bag, but do not overfill. Pull the open end of the casing up over the tip of the piping bag, gathering it as much as possible. Gently stuff the casing with the meat filling, being careful not to split the casing, and leaving some extra space so the rice can expand as it cooks. Every 6 to 8 inches (15–20cm), twist the casing a few times to form a link. When you reach the end of the casing, tie another knot to finish it off. When ready to cook, cut through the twists to separate the links.

4. Place the fawaregh in a large pot with water to cover. Set over high heat, and bring to a boil, discarding the fat that rises to the top as it cooks.

5. Add the onions, bay leaves, cardamom, remaining 1 teaspoon salt, cloves, and black peppercorns. Cover, and simmer for 1 hour. Serve hot.

Lahm bi Ajeen

MINI MEAT PIES

PREP TIME: **40 MINUTES**	COOK TIME: **10 MINUTES**	TOTAL TIME: **50 MINUTES**

SERVES: 6

VEGAN (substitute vegan meat alternative)

Also known as sfiha, these are traditional mini Lebanese meat pies shaped in different ways. Lahm bi Ajeen are filled with a seasoned ground beef mixture and are impressive enough to serve for large groups, parties, or special occasions.

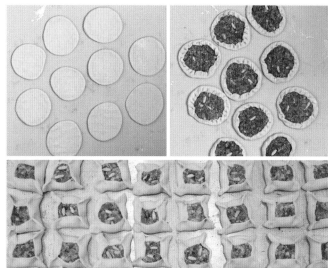

ingredients:

1 batch **Al Ajeen (Basic Dough; page 232)**

Lemon

FILLING:

3 medium tomatoes (417g), chopped

1 medium yellow onion (156g), chopped

1 lb (500g) finely minced lean ground beef
(80% lean/20% fat) or mixture of lamb and beef

1 tsp salt

1 tsp **Lebanese 7 Spices (page 261)**

½ tsp red chili powder

2 tbsp olive oil

1½ tbsp pine nuts (optional)

note:

If you like your Lahm bi Ajeen to taste fattier, you
can use lamb meat or half lamb and half lean beef.

1. To make the meat filling, in a food processor, blend the tomatoes and onion until smooth. (Or chop them very finely using a grater or a knife.) Strain the mixture through a fine mesh sieve to remove the excess liquid. This is a crucial step to avoid a soggy meat mixture that could unravel the pies during baking.

2. Transfer the minced tomatoes and onion mixture to a large bowl, and add the minced meat, salt, Lebanese 7 Spices, red chili powder, olive oil, and pine nuts (if using). Mix well into a homogeneous mixture.

3. To make the pie crusts, flour a countertop and break off pieces of the Al Ajeen dough into equal balls almost the size of ping-pong balls. Using a rolling pin, roll out each dough ball to a circle 4 inches (10cm) in diameter and ¼ inch (0.5cm) thick.

4. Preheat the oven to 400°F (200°C), and place the rack in the center of the oven. Lightly brush a baking sheet with a little oil.

5. Place 1 tablespoon of the meat filling in the center of each dough circle. Pinch the adjacent sides of the dough, creating a square shape, as shown in the photo at the left. Or pinch the contour of the dough, as shown in the photo at the top right.

6. Place the pies on the oiled baking sheet, avoiding overcrowding. Bake for about 10 minutes or until the crust is golden.

7. Serve warm with a squeeze of lemon. Enjoy with some Laban Ayran (Salted Yogurt Drink; page 219).

Chicken & Fish

Shawarma Djaj

CHICKEN SHAWARMA

PREP TIME: **10 MINUTES**
+ 4 hours (marinating)

COOK TIME: **15 MINUTES**

TOTAL TIME: **25 MINUTES**
+ marinating

SERVES: 4

VEGAN (substitute vegan meat & yogurt alternatives)

This easy-to-prepare chicken dish is tasty on its own, but it's also great tucked into a pita bread for a sandwich or an on-the-go meal.

ingredients:

1⅓ lb (600g) boneless, skinless chicken thigh fillets

MARINADE:

2 tbsp freshly squeezed lemon juice

½ cup (125g) plain full-fat yogurt

¾ cup (178ml) vegetable oil

1 medium yellow onion (170g), thinly sliced

CHICKEN SHAWARMA SPICE:

½ tsp ground coriander

½ tsp ground ginger

1 tsp ground cardamom

1½ tsp smoked paprika

½ tsp salt

1 tsp black pepper

½ tsp white pepper

1 tbsp garlic powder

TO SERVE:

Potato fries

Pita bread

Kabis (Pickles; page 246)

Tomatoes

Lettuce

Toum (Garlic Sauce; page 248)

storage:

Store any leftovers in an airtight container in the refrigerator for up to 5 days, or freeze for up to 3 months.

1. Make the marinade and chicken shawarma spice. In a large bowl, whisk together the lemon juice, yogurt, oil, onion, coriander, ginger, cardamom, paprika, salt, black pepper, white pepper, and garlic powder.

2. Cut the chicken into thin slices, add to the marinade, and stir well to evenly coat. Cover the bowl, and marinate in the refrigerator for at least 4 hours or overnight.

3. In a large sauté pan over medium heat, sauté the chicken for about 10 to 15 minutes, flipping over once or twice, until deep golden and cooked.

4. Serve with fries or in a pita bread as a sandwich with fries, Kabis, tomatoes, lettuce, and Toum.

Molokhia bi Aldjaj

JUTE MALLOW WITH CHICKEN

| PREP TIME: **1 HOUR** | COOK TIME: **40 MINUTES** | TOTAL TIME: **1 HOUR 40 MINUTES** |

SERVES: 4–5

VEGAN (substitute vegan meat alternative & vegetable broth)

You won't believe the inviting aroma of jute leaves, cilantro, lemon, and garlic that fills your kitchen as you make this meal that's guaranteed to impress. The preparation may be a bit lengthy, but it'll be worth every minute when you taste it.

ingredients:

190g (7oz) dried jute mallow (molokhia yabseh), minced

½ cup (120ml) freshly squeezed lemon juice

½ cup (120ml) vegetable oil

1 tbsp coriander seeds, crushed

3 small heads garlic (90g), peeled and minced, divided

2 bunches fresh cilantro, chopped, divided

1 small red chili pepper (11g), chopped

1 tsp salt

1 lb (515g) meat from 2 lb (1kg) chicken, boiled (see note)

4 cups (1 liter) chicken broth

Riz bi Sh'arieh (Rice with Vermicelli; page 241)

Lemon slices

note:

To boil the chicken and make broth, place the chicken in a large pot, add 6 to 8 cups (1.4–1.9 liters) water or to fully cover, and set over high heat. Bring to a boil, skimming off any foam that rises to the top. Add 1 small halved yellow onion, 3 cloves garlic, 1 small cinnamon stick, 1 bay leaf, 9 cardamom pods, 4 whole cloves, 1 teaspoon black peppercorns, and 1 tablespoon salt. Cover, reduce heat to low, and simmer for 1 hour. To use, remove chicken from the pot, and strain and reserve the broth.

1. Clean the jute leaves well, and soak them in hot water and lemon juice for 1 hour. Rinse well until the water turns clear and then squeeze the jute using the palms of your hands until it's very dry.

2. In a large pot over medium-high heat, heat the oil. Add the jute in batches with some crushed coriander seeds, and fry for 3 or 4 minutes per batch or until jute is very dry, a little crisp, and turns a deep green color.

3. In a separate large pot over medium-low heat, fry ¾ of the garlic for 2 minutes. Add ¾ of the chopped cilantro and all of the red chili pepper, and stir well.

4. Add the fried jute and salt, and stir-fry for 2 minutes.

5. Add the chicken and chicken broth, cover, reduce heat to low, and simmer for 30 minutes.

6. Add the rest of the minced garlic and the chopped cilantro to the jute, and cook for 2 more minutes.

7. Serve hot with Riz bi Sh'arieh and lemon slices.

storage:

Store any leftovers in an airtight container in the refrigerator for up to 5 days, or freeze for up to 3 months.

Hareesa

CHICKEN WHEAT PORRIDGE

PREP TIME: **10 MINUTES** + 12 hours (soaking)	COOK TIME: **3½ HOURS**	TOTAL TIME: **4 HOURS** + soaking

SERVES: 8

VEGAN (substitute vegan meat alternative & vegetable broth)

Warm, rich, and delicious, this creamy soup has the comforting consistency of porridge—no wonder it's a staple in Lebanon. Hareesa is well known in Lebanese villages as a charity dish, served on Ashura occasions. It's cooked in a large, communal pot and shared.

ingredients:

5½ cups (1kg) pearled wheat (wheat berries)

1 tsp baking soda

14 cups (3.3 liters) water

4 lb (2kg) boiled and shredded chicken (page 228)

8½ cups (2 liters) chicken broth (page 228)

1 tbsp salt

½ tsp ground mistiki (mastic powder)

1 cup (250g) melted butter

Ground cinnamon

storage:

Store any leftovers in an airtight container in the refrigerator for up to 5 days, or freeze for up to 3 months.

notes:

To ensure the correct consistency of the Hareesa, for every 5½ cups (1kg) pearled wheat, you need 4 pounds (2kg) cooked, shredded chicken.

Adding baking soda to the soak water helps the pearled wheat cook faster.

1. Wash the pearled wheat, and place in a large bowl. Add the baking soda and enough water to cover, and soak for at least 12 hours or overnight.

2. After soaking, wash the wheat well again. Place in a large pot, add the water, set over medium-high heat, and bring to a boil. Reduce the heat to medium-low, cover, and simmer for 2 or 3 hours or until the wheat is tender and soft. If you're using a pressure cooker, cook for about 1 hour or until the wheat is very tender.

3. Add the chicken, chicken broth, salt, mistiki, and melted butter to the wheat, and stir well. Cook, stirring constantly, over low heat for about 30 minutes, crushing the wheat and chicken using the bottom of your ladle so they get very soft. Alternatively, you can use a food processor or an immersion blender to give the cooked mixture a few short pulses until it has a chunky-smooth texture—not too smooth and not too chunky.

4. Serve hot on a plate with a sprinkle of cinnamon.

Moghrabieh

LEBANESE COUSCOUS

PREP TIME: **10 MINUTES**	COOK TIME: **1 HOUR 45 MINUTES**	TOTAL TIME: **2 HOURS**

SERVES: 6

VEGAN (substitute vegan meat alternative)

This traditional Lebanese couscous is warm and satisfying—just what you need to warm up on a cold night. The rich, spicy flavors and tender chicken appeal even to picky eaters.

ingredients:

2 lb (1kg) chicken drumsticks (about 7)

12½ cups (3 liters) water

1 small yellow onion (125g), halved

3 cloves garlic

1 small cinnamon stick

1 bay leaf

4 whole cloves

9 cardamom pods

1 tsp black peppercorns

1 tbsp salt

2 tbsp ghee

8–10 pearl onions, peeled, or 1 medium yellow onion (240g), quartered

2 cups (382g) cooked chickpeas

1 tsp ground caraway

½ tsp ground cinnamon

½ tsp ground allspice

2 cups (410g) dried giant couscous

storage:

Store in an airtight container in the refrigerator for up to 3 days. When reheating, add more water because the couscous will have absorbed the original water.

note:

If you want to use 3 cups (390g) fresh couscous instead of the dry, you do not have to boil it in step 5. Add it to the ghee used to fry the onions, and stir-fry as directed.

1. Place the chicken in a large pot, add 9 cups (2.3 liters) water or to fully cover, and set over high heat. Bring to a boil, skimming off any foam that rises to the top. Add the small yellow onion, garlic, cinnamon stick, bay leaf, cloves, cardamom, black peppercorns, and salt. Cover, reduce heat to low, and simmer for 1 hour.

2. In a separate large pot over medium-high heat, heat the ghee. Add the pearl onions, and fry for 5 minutes or until translucent and golden. Remove the onions from the pan, leaving the ghee.

3. Add the cooked chickpeas and the fried pearl onions to the chicken and broth, and simmer for 10 minutes.

4. Prepare the spice mix by combining the caraway, cinnamon, and allspice.

5. In a medium pan over medium-high heat, bring the remaining 3½ cups (875ml) water and dried couscous to a boil, and cook for 10 minutes. Drain. In the same ghee used to fry the onions, add the boiled couscous, and stir-fry over very low heat for 2 minutes. (If using fresh couscous, skip the boiling, and stir-fry it in the ghee used to fry the onions over very low heat for 5 minutes.) Add the spice mix to the couscous, and stir.

6. Reduce the heat to low, and gradually add several ladles of chicken broth (6 cups/1.4 liters) to the couscous, being careful not to get the bay leaf or any of the whole spices. Simmer gently, stirring occasionally with a wooden spoon, for about 10 minutes or until the grains are soft and the couscous has absorbed the flavors.

7. Add the chickpeas, chicken, and pearl onions along with more broth to thin if you like. Stir, simmer for another 5 minutes, and serve hot.

Freekeh with Chicken

ROASTED GREEN WHEAT & CHICKEN

PREP TIME: **10 MINUTES** + 1 hour (soaking)	COOK TIME: **50 MINUTES**	TOTAL TIME: **1 HOUR** + soaking

SERVES: 10–12

VEGAN (substitute vegan meat alternative & vegetable broth)

Freekeh is an ancient green wheat grain. This hearty recipe makes a delicious and healthy traditional Lebanese meal, full of flavor and high in protein and fiber.

ingredients:

3 cups (500g) freekeh

3⅓ lb (1.5kg) chicken thighs

¼ cup (60ml) vegetable oil

1⅓ cups (200g) mixed nuts (almonds, pine nuts, pistachios, cashews), or ⅓ cup (50g) each

2 medium yellow onions (340g), chopped

1 tsp salt

½ tsp black pepper

1 tsp sweet paprika

4 cups (1 liter) chicken broth

MARINADE:

½ cup (120ml) olive oil

Juice of 2 large lemons (½ cup/120ml)

1 tsp sweet paprika

½ tbsp salt

1 tsp black pepper

1 tsp ground cardamom

1 tsp ground coriander

1 tsp ground ginger

3 cloves garlic, finely minced

1. Soak the freekeh in hot water for 1 hour.

2. Meanwhile, make the marinade. In a small bowl, combine the olive oil, lemon juice, 1 teaspoon paprika, ½ tablespoon salt, 1 teaspoon pepper, cardamom, coriander, ginger, and garlic. Rub the mixture all over each chicken thigh, and marinate in the refrigerator for at least 30 minutes.

3. Preheat the oven to 400°F (200°C).

4. Transfer the marinated chicken to a baking sheet, and bake for 35 to 40 minutes. Turn on the broiler, and cook the chicken for 5 more minutes or until it's golden brown on top.

5. After 1 hour, strain the freekeh and set it aside.

6. In a small pan over medium heat, heat the vegetable oil. Add the different nuts in small batches, and fry, stirring, for 3 or 4 minutes or until golden. When all the nuts are cooked, set them aside.

7. In a deep pot, and using the oil used to fry the nuts, cook the onions for 5 minutes or until they become light brown. Add the freekeh, remaining 1 teaspoon salt, remaining ½ teaspoon pepper, and remaining 1 teaspoon paprika, and stir-fry for 3 minutes.

8. Add the chicken broth, and bring to a boil over medium-high heat. Stir, reduce the heat to low, cover, and cook for 20 minutes or until the freekeh is fluffy and tender. Uncover and stir a couple times to prevent the freekeh from sticking to the pot.

9. Serve on a shallow plate, with the chicken over the freekeh and topped with the fried nuts.

Shorbet Djaj

CHICKEN SOUP

PREP TIME: **10 MINUTES**	COOK TIME: **20 MINUTES**	TOTAL TIME: **30 MINUTES**

SERVES: 3

VEGAN (substitute vegan meat alternative)

GLUTEN FREE

Warm up cold days with this hearty chicken soup that's full of vegetables, rice, and a flavorful broth that hits the spot for lunch or for dinner.

ingredients:

8 cups (2 liters) chicken broth (page 228)

1 cup (200g) short-grain rice, washed well, rinsed, and drained

1 medium carrot (85g), chopped

1–2 stalks celery (95g), chopped

2 cups (200g) boiled and shredded chicken (page 228)

½ cup (104g) diced tomatoes

1 cup (28g) fresh flat-leaf parsley, chopped

Salt (optional)

Lemon

storage:

Store any leftovers in an airtight container in the refrigerator for up to 5 days, or freeze for up to 3 months.

1. In a large pot over high heat, bring the chicken broth to a boil. Gradually add the rice, carrot, celery, and chicken. Reduce the heat to low, cover, and simmer for 15 minutes.

2. Add the tomatoes and parsley at the end. Season with salt (if using), stir, and simmer for 2 more minutes.

3. To serve, ladle into bowls and top with a squeeze of lemon juice.

Djej w Batata

CHICKEN & POTATOES

PREP TIME: **15 MINUTES**
+ 1 hour (marinating, optional)

COOK TIME: **1 HOUR**

TOTAL TIME: **1 HOUR 15 MINUTES**
+ marinating

SERVES: 4–6

VEGAN (substitute vegan meat alternative)

GLUTEN FREE

After an hour in the oven, the chicken and potatoes in this traditional dish, full of aromatic seasonings and rich in protein, become irresistibly soft and tender.

ingredients:

2 cups (35g) fresh cilantro leaves, chopped, divided

1 head garlic (30g), peeled and thinly sliced, divided

1 small red chili pepper (12g), thinly sliced, divided

1½ lb (704g) chicken drumsticks

3 large russet potatoes (1kg), cut into thin rounds about ½ in (1.25cm) thick

½ cup freshly squeezed lemon juice

½ cup (120ml) vegetable oil

3 bay leaves

8 cardamom pods

1 tsp coriander seeds

1 tsp black pepper

1½ tsp salt

Lemon slices

note:

For an extra-hearty meal, serve with Riz bi Sh'arieh (Rice with Vermicelli; page 241).

1. In a large bowl, combine ¾ of each of the cilantro, garlic, and red chili pepper with the chicken, potato rounds, lemon juice, oil, bay leaves, cardamom, coriander seeds, pepper, and salt. Mix well, and if you have the time, marinate in the refrigerator for 1 hour.

2. Preheat the oven to 350°F (180°C).

3. Arrange the chicken and potato mixture on a baking sheet, cover with foil, and bake for 45 minutes to 1 hour or until the potatoes are soft and cooked through. Remove the bay leaves.

4. In a small saucepan over medium-high heat, fry the remaining cilantro, garlic, and red chili pepper. Use as garnish over the chicken and potatoes. Add lemon slices, and serve.

Farrouj Meshwi

ROASTED CHICKEN

| PREP TIME: **10 MINUTES** | COOK TIME: **1 HOUR 10 MINUTES** | TOTAL TIME: **1 HOUR 20 MINUTES** |

SERVES: 5
GLUTEN FREE

Farrouj Meshwi is the ultimate traditional restaurant dish that appeals to the whole family. It's perfect on Riz bi Sh'arieh (Rice with Vermicelli; page 241) and delicious with Toum (Garlic Sauce; page 248).

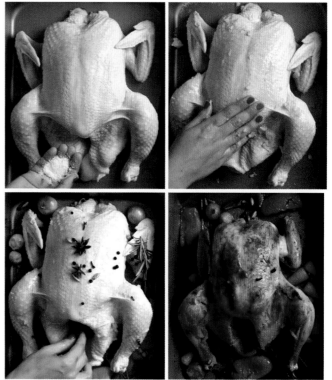

ingredients:

4½ lb (2kg) whole chicken

1 tbsp salt

¼ cup (60ml) freshly squeezed lemon juice

1½ tbsp apple cider vinegar or white vinegar

4 cloves garlic, minced

3 tbsp grated ginger (1- or 2-in/2.5–5cm piece)

2 bay leaves

1 tsp ground cardamom

½ tbsp black peppercorns

2 star anise pods

½ tsp whole cloves

2 cinnamon sticks

2 medium carrots (200g)

A few sprigs of fresh rosemary (16g)

2 stalks celery (90g)

1 red bell pepper (120g), ribs and seeds removed, and sliced

1 medium yellow onion (170g)

¾ cup (100g) melted butter

4 cups (1 liter) water

1. Preheat the oven to 400°F (200°C).

2. Place the chicken in a roasting pan, and season it inside and outside with the salt, lemon juice, vinegar, garlic, and ginger.

3. Do the same with the whole spices, sprinkling the bay leaves, cardamom, black peppercorns, star anise pods, cloves, and cinnamon sticks inside and outside the chicken.

4. Stuff the carrots into the cavity of the chicken along with the rosemary, celery, bell pepper, and onion.

5. Brush the chicken with the melted butter, pour the water in the pan around the chicken, and cover with foil. Roast for 45 minutes.

6. Remove the cover. Drain and reserve the broth for another use. Return the chicken to the oven, and roast, uncovered, for 20 more minutes. Turn on the broiler, and broil for 5 minutes or until golden.

7. Serve warm. Enjoy with Toum (Garlic Sauce; page 248) or Riz bi Sh'arieh (Rice with Vermicelli; page 241).

Samke Harra

SPICY BAKED FISH

| PREP TIME: **10 MINUTES** | COOK TIME: **30 MINUTES** | TOTAL TIME: **40 MINUTES** |

SERVES: 3–4
GLUTEN FREE

This flavorful fish dish is often served for Lebanese special occasions. You'll love how the flesh turns out so spicy and juicy.

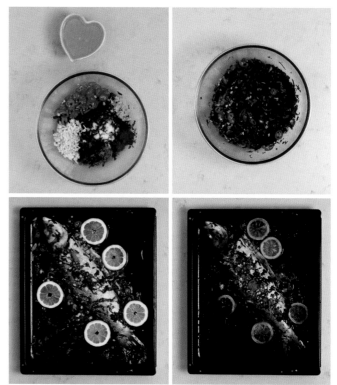

ingredients:

1 cup (16g) fresh cilantro, coarsely chopped

⅓ cup (30g) walnuts, coarsely chopped

1 long red chili pepper (50g), coarsely chopped

2–3 small red-eye chili peppers (6g), coarsely chopped

½ in (1.25cm) piece fresh ginger (9g), peeled and minced

10 cloves garlic (50g), coarsely chopped

½ tbsp salt

1 tsp ground cumin

1 tsp sweet paprika

½ cup (125ml) freshly squeezed lemon juice

½ cup (125ml) vegetable oil

2 lb (1kg) snapper fish

Lemon slices

Taratur (Tahini Sauce; page 251)

Lemon wedges

1. In a large bowl, combine the cilantro, walnuts, chili peppers, ginger, and garlic. Add the salt, cumin, paprika, lemon juice, and oil, and mix well.

2. Preheat the oven to 375°F (190°C).

3. Make three slits from top to bottom on each side of the fish with a knife, and rub the fish with the spice mixture, being sure to get inside the slits and the cavity of the fish, too.

4. Place the fish on a baking sheet with some lemon slices, and cover with foil. Roast for 25 to 30 minutes or until the fish reaches an internal temperature of 145°F to 150°F (63°C–65°C) on a meat thermometer.

5. Serve with Taratur and lemon wedges.

Sayadeyieh

LEBANESE FISH & RICE

PREP TIME: **15 MINUTES**	COOK TIME: **30 MINUTES**	TOTAL TIME: **45 MINUTES**

SERVES: 4
GLUTEN FREE

Sweet, caramelized rice brings instant comfort and pairs wonderfully with seasoned, flaky cod. Enjoy with Lebanese Salata (Tomato Cucumber Salad; page 49) for a tasty meal.

ingredients:

1½ tbsp ground cumin, divided

½ tsp ground ginger

1 cup (250ml) vegetable oil, divided

1 lb (765g) cod fillets

1 medium yellow onion (170g), cut into rings

1 large yellow onion (190g), chopped

2 cups (370g) yellow long-grain rice

2½ cups (500ml) shellfish stock or water

TO SERVE:

Taratur (Tahini Sauce; page 251)

⅓ cup (50g) pine nuts, toasted

1½ cups crispy fried onions

¼ cup (15g) fresh flat-leaf parsley, chopped

Lemon wedges

note:

If using water instead of the shellfish stock, add ½ tablespoon salt. I don't add salt to the rice because the shellfish stock contains enough already.

1. Preheat the oven to 350°F (180°C).

2. In a small bowl, combine ½ tablespoon cumin, the ginger, and ½ cup (125ml) oil. Evenly massage the spice mixture on both sides of the fish fillets. Place the fish on a baking sheet, and surround with the onion rings. Bake for 25 to 30 minutes or until the fish becomes flaky and cooked through.

3. Meanwhile, rinse the rice several times until the water runs clear. Drain.

4. In a large pot over medium-high heat, heat the remaining ½ cup (125ml) oil. Add the chopped onions, and cook, stirring occasionally, for 10 minutes or until the onions have caramelized into a deep golden brown.

5. Add the rice and remaining 1 tablespoon cumin, and stir-fry for 2 minutes. Add the shellfish stock (or water), and bring to boil. Cover, reduce the heat to low, and cook for 15 minutes or until all the liquid has been absorbed.

6. Serve the rice and fish on a bed of Taratur, garnished with toasted pine nuts, crispy fried onions, chopped parsley, and lemon wedges.

Kabsi Rice
RICE & CHICKEN

PREP TIME: **5 MINUTES**	COOK TIME: **45 MINUTES**	TOTAL TIME: **50 MINUTES**

SERVES: 6
GLUTEN FREE

Quick and simple, Kabsi Rice is the perfect base for almost any Lebanese meal, and it can be the star of your family dinner. It pairs especially well with Farrouj Meshwi (Roasted Chicken; page 142).

ingredients:

3 cups (570g) basmati rice

¼ cup (60ml) vegetable oil

1 large yellow onion (190g), chopped

1 tbsp **Kabsi Spice Blend (page 263)**

1 tbsp salt (optional)

3½ cups (875ml) chicken stock, vegetable stock, or water

1 cup (150g) mixed nuts (pistachios, pine nuts, cashews, blanched almonds, etc.)

Farrouj Meshwi (Roasted Chicken; page 142)

¼ cup (15g) chopped fresh flat-leaf parsley

note:

If you don't want to fry the nuts in oil, you can dry-roast them in a sauté pan over medium heat. Roast the pistachios for 10 minutes, the pine nuts for 3 minutes, the cashews for 5 minutes, and the blanched almonds for 4 minutes. Be careful not to let them burn.

1. Rinse the rice several times until the water runs clear. Drain.

2. In a large pot over medium-high heat, heat the oil. Add the onion, and sauté for 3 minutes or until the onion softens and turns golden. Add the Kabsi Spice Blend, and fry for 1 minute.

3. Add the rice, season with salt if using unsalted stock or water, and sauté for 1 minute. Add the stock, and bring to a boil. Reduce the heat to low, cover, and simmer for about 10 minutes.

4. Remove the lid, cover with a cotton cloth, and cook for 5 minutes. Turn off the heat, and let the rice rest for 10 to 15 minutes. The cotton will absorb the vapor so the rice will be fluffy and not stuck together. Fluff the rice with a fork to break up any clumps.

5. In a small pan over medium heat, heat a little more vegetable oil. Add the different nuts separately, and fry, stirring, for 3 or 4 minutes or until golden.

6. Serve the rice with the Farrouj Meshwi and fried nuts on top and garnished with parsley.

Barbecue

Shish Tawook

CHICKEN SKEWERS

PREP TIME: **10 MINUTES** + 6 hours (marinating)	COOK TIME: **10 MINUTES**	TOTAL TIME: **20 MINUTES** + marinating

MAKES: 30 skewers

GLUTEN FREE (omit pita)

These grilled chicken skewers, and the following barbecued meat and vegetable recipes (mashawi), are delicious Lebanese staples. They're often made in large amounts for parties or family picnics, and they're almost always cooked on a charcoal grill.

ingredients:

5 lb (2.3kg) boneless, skinless chicken breast

MARINADE:

¼ cup (245g) plain full-fat yogurt

¾ cup (200ml) vegetable oil

1 tbsp apple cider vinegar

1½ tsp yellow mustard

2 tbsp sweet paprika

1½ tbsp salt

2 tsp white pepper

TO SERVE:

Pita bread

¼ cup (100g) **Toum (Garlic Sauce; page 248)**

Tomatoes, sliced

Cucumber **Kabis (Pickles; page 246)**

Lettuce

storage:

Store any leftovers in an airtight container in the refrigerator for up to 3 or 4 days, or freeze for up to 3 months.

notes:

You can make the chicken ahead and freeze the marinated cubes. Use them within 2 months.

1. In a large bowl, prepare the marinade by whisking together the yogurt, oil, vinegar, mustard, paprika, salt, and pepper.

2. Cut the chicken breasts into 1-inch (2.5cm) cubes, add to the marinade, and toss to coat. Cover and refrigerate for at least 6 hours or overnight to marinate.

3. Preheat the grill to 350°F (175°C).

4. Thread the chicken cubes onto metal skewers, and grill for 8 to 10 minutes, rotating every 2 or 3 minutes, until the chicken reaches an internal temperature of 165°F (75°C).

5. Serve hot with pita bread, Toum, tomatoes, cucumber Kabis, and lettuce.

Kafta Skewers

GRILLED LEBANESE KEBABS

PREP TIME: **10 MINUTES**
+ 30 minutes (marinating)

COOK TIME: **10 MINUTES**

TOTAL TIME: **20 MINUTES**
+ marinating

MAKES: 12 skewers

GLUTEN FREE (omit pita)

These ground meat skewers can be made with lamb or beef. If you don't have wide kafta skewers, you can cook the formed meat on the top grate of the grill.

ingredients:

2 lb (875g) ground lamb or beef (80% lean/20% fat)

1¾ cups (47g) fresh flat-leaf parsley, chopped

¾ cup (155g) chopped yellow onion

2 tsp **Lebanese 7 Spices (page 261)**

1 tbsp salt

2 tsp black pepper

TO SERVE:

Pita bread

Hummus bi Tahini (Hummus; page 32)

Chili paste

Kabis (Pickles; page 246)

Chili pitta

Salatet Bakdounes (Parsley Onion Salad; page 63)

Grilled vegetables (page 157)

1. In a large bowl, combine the ground meat, parsley, onion, Lebanese 7 Spices, salt, and pepper. Refrigerate for at least 30 minutes.

2. Using your hands, form about ½ cup (85–100g) of the mixture on and around the skewers, pressing firmly so it doesn't fall off.

3. Preheat the grill to 350°F (175°C).

4. Add the skewers to the grill, and cook for 8 to 10 minutes, turning once, until the meat reaches an internal temperature of 160°F (70°C).

5. Serve hot with pita bread, Hummus bi Tahini, chili paste, Kabis, chili pitta, Salatet Bakdounes, and grilled vegetables.

Lahem Meshwi

LAMB SKEWERS

PREP TIME: **10 MINUTES**
+ 30 minutes (marinating)

COOK TIME: **10 MINUTES**

TOTAL TIME: **20 MINUTES**
+ marinating

MAKES: 3 skewers

GLUTEN FREE

ingredients:

1⅓ lb (600g) lamb

6 small shallots (400g), halved

2 tsp olive oil

1 tsp chili paste

½ tsp salt

1 tsp black pepper

TO SERVE:

Grilled vegetables (page 157)

Hummus bi Tahini (Hummus; page 32)

Marinated lamb and shallots are grilled to tender, flavorful perfection.

1. Cut the lamb into medium-size (1- or 2-inch/2.5–5cm) cubes, and place in a large bowl. Add the shallots, oil, chili paste, salt, and pepper, and mix well. Refrigerate for at least 30 minutes.

2. Preheat the grill to 350°F (175°C).

3. Thread the lamb and shallots onto metal skewers, and grill for 8 to 10 minutes, turning once, until the meat reaches an internal temperature of 160°F (70°C).

4. Serve hot with grilled vegetables and Hummus bi Tahini or your favorite dip.

Mashawi
MIXED BARBECUE

PREP TIME: **5 MINUTES**	COOK TIME: **10 MINUTES**	TOTAL TIME: **15 MINUTES**

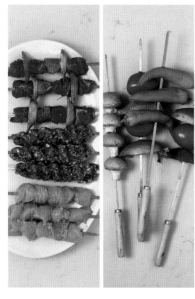

MAKES: 30 Shish Tawook, 12 Kafta Skewers, & 3 Lahem Meshwi, plus grilled vegetables

ingredients:

Whole brown button mushrooms, halved shallots, whole small tomatoes, whole hot chili peppers

Salt

TO SERVE:

Kafta Skewers (Grilled Lebanese Kebabs; page 154)

Shish Tawook (Chicken Skewers; page 152)

Lahem Meshwi (Lamb Skewers; page 156)

Tabbouleh (page 28)

Hummus bi Tahini (Hummus; page 32)

Moutabal (Eggplant Dip; page 36)

Salatet Bakdounes (Parsley Onion Salad; page 63)

Laymonada (Mint Lemonade; page 218)

Pita bread

Lemon slices

For a true barbecue feast, prepare all the recipes in this section and serve with grilled vegetables and other Lebanese favorites. (Adjust the amounts as you like.)

1. To make the grilled vegetables, preheat the grill to 350°F (175°C).

2. Thread your choice of vegetables onto metal skewers, sprinkle with salt, and grill for about 10 minutes, turning once, until charred.

3. Serve hot with Kafta Skewers, Shish Tawook, Lahem Meshwi, Tabbouleh, Hummus bi Tahini, Moutabal, Salatet Bakdounes, Laymonada, pita bread, and lemon slices.

Vegetarian

Falafel

| PREP TIME: **10 MINUTES**
+ 8 hours (soaking) | COOK TIME: **10 MINUTES** | TOTAL TIME: **20 MINUTES**
+ soaking |

MAKES: 20 falafel balls

VEGAN

The epitome of Beirut street food, this is my favorite falafel around Lebanon. Whether you want falafel balls or falafel sandwiches, this recipe yields delicious, crispy-on-the-outside, soft-on-the-inside falafel.

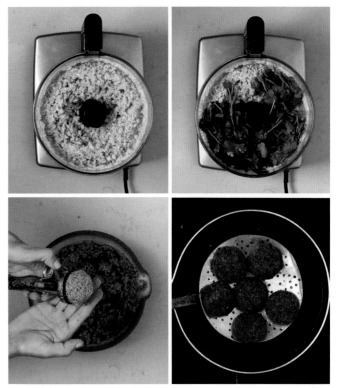

ingredients:

4 cups (816g) dried
chickpeas

1 medium yellow onion
(140g)

3 cloves garlic (18g)

1½ cups (45g) fresh
cilantro leaves

1½ cups (45g) fresh flat-
leaf parsley leaves

1 tbsp **Falafel Spice
(page 262)**

½ tsp salt

½ tsp baking powder

4–5 cups (1–1.2 liters)
sunflower oil, for
frying

storage:

You can prepare the falafel
mixture in advance and
store it, covered, in the
refrigerator for up to
4 days, or freeze it for
up to 3 months.

TO SERVE:

**Taratur (Tahini Sauce;
page 251)**

**Cucumber or turnip
Kabis (Pickles;
page 246)**

Tomatoes

Lettuce, chopped

Fresh flat-leaf parsley,
chopped

Pita bread

notes:

If the falafel dough isn't
holding together or is too
wet, you can add chickpea
flour, in small amounts at
a time, during step 2. If
it's not holding together
or is too dry, add water,
again in small amounts
at a time.

If you like sesame seeds,
you can coat the falafel
balls with 2 tablespoons
just before frying.

1. Soak the dried chickpeas overnight or for at least
   8 hours. Drain and rinse well.

2. In a food processor, roughly chop the onion and garlic.
   Add the chickpeas, and blitz to crumbs. Add the cilantro
   and parsley, and process to get a homogenous mixture.
   Pour the mixture into a large bowl, add the Falafel Spice
   and salt, and mix with a spoon.

3. If you're ready to make the falafel now, add the baking
   powder, mix, and wait 30 minutes before frying.
   Otherwise, refrigerate or freeze the mixture.

4. In a large saucepan over high heat, heat a few inches
   of oil until it bubbles softly (350°F/180°C). Working
   in batches, form the patties using a falafel scoop or
   a spoon. Carefully place the patties in the hot oil,
   and cook for 3 or 4 minutes. Turn over, and cook the
   other side until golden brown. Using a slotted spoon,
   transfer the falafel to paper towels to drain.

5. Serve hot as part of a mezze platter with Taratur, Kabis,
   tomatoes, lettuce, parsley, and pita bread. Or make
   into a pita wrap with the Taratur, tomato, cucumber
   or turnip Kabis, lettuce, and parsley.

Kibbeh Laktin

PUMPKIN KIBBEH

PREP TIME: **15 MINUTES**	COOK TIME: **1 HOUR**	TOTAL TIME: **1 HOUR 15 MINUTES**

SERVES: 3
VEGAN

Kibbeh Laktin is a mouthwatering pumpkin dish—like a fancy vegan kibbeh. The pumpkin purée comes together with the bulgur so easily. You can replace the fresh pumpkin with canned pumpkin if you like.

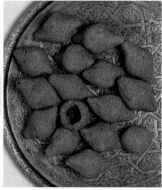

ingredients:

1 medium pumpkin (enough for 3 cups/713g purée)

3 cups (492g) fine **Bulgur Wheat (Crushed Wheat; page 242)**

2 tsp **Kamouneh Spice Blend (page 264)**

½ tsp ground cinnamon

1 tsp salt

½ cup flour (optional)

Taratur (Tahini Sauce; page 251)

FILLING:

2 tbsp vegetable oil, plus more for deep-frying

1 medium yellow onion (140g), finely chopped

1 cup (167g) cooked chickpeas

4 cups (125g) spinach or Swiss chard, chopped

1 tsp ground sumac

2 tbsp **Debs al Romman (Pomegranate Molasses; page 253)**

1 tsp salt

1 tsp **Lebanese 7 Spices (page 261)**

1. Preheat the oven to 375°F (190°C). Line a baking sheet with parchment paper.

2. Cut the pumpkin in half lengthwise, and scrape out the seeds and strings. Place the pumpkin flesh side down on the baking sheet, and pierce the skin a few times with a fork or knife. Bake for 45 minutes or until a fork easily pierces the skin. Remove from the oven, and cool for 10 minutes. Scoop out the flesh, purée in a blender until creamy, and transfer 3 cups (713g) to a large bowl.

3. Add the Bulgur Wheat, Kamouneh Spice Blend, cinnamon, and 1 teaspoon salt. Mash together using your hands until no pumpkin lumps remain. (If the mixture is not holding together, add some flour.)

4. Make the filling. In a large pan over medium-high heat, heat 2 tablespoons oil. Add the onion, and stir-fry for 5 minutes. Add the chickpeas and spinach, and cook for 2 minutes. Add the sumac, Debs al Romman, remaining 1 teaspoon salt, and Lebanese 7 Spices. Cook for 1 minute, remove from heat, and set aside to cool.

5. Wet your hands with water and then scoop about 3 tablespoons of the kibbeh mixture. Form into an oblong ball and then hollow out the inside using your finger until it looks like a half shell. Add about 2 tablespoons filling to the shell, press the shell closed, and shape it into a classic kibbeh. Set on a tray, and repeat with the remaining mixture.

6. In a large saucepan over high heat, heat a few inches of oil until it bubbles softly (350°F/180°C). Working in batches, deep-fry the kibbeh for 2 or 3 minutes or until golden brown and crisp. Using a slotted spoon, carefully transfer the kibbeh to paper towels to drain.

7. Serve hot with Taratur or a salad.

Maghmour/Moussaka

EGGPLANT & CHICKPEA STEW

PREP TIME: **10 MINUTES** + 1 hour (straining)	COOK TIME: **25 MINUTES**	TOTAL TIME: **35 MINUTES** + straining

SERVES: 4–5

VEGAN

GLUTEN FREE

This dish might contain humble ingredients, but the flavor is anything but! The eggplant's sweet and mild flavor combines beautifully with the other hearty ingredients to spark the appetite.

1. Chop the eggplants into 1- or 2-inch (2.5–5cm) cubes all about the same size so they'll cook evenly. Rub the cubes with ½ teaspoon salt, place them in a strainer on top of a large bowl, and set aside for 1 hour.

2. Meanwhile, in a large frying pan over medium-high heat, heat ¼ cup (60ml) oil. Add the onions and garlic, and sauté for 2 or 3 minutes.

3. Add the tomatoes, tomato paste, remaining ½ tablespoon salt, black pepper, Lebanese 7 Spices, and chili pepper. Stir to incorporate, cover, reduce the heat to low, and simmer for about 15 minutes.

4. In a large, deep saucepan over high heat, heat some vegetable oil. Add the eggplant cubes in small batches, and fry for 2 to 4 minutes, turning often, until golden and crispy. Transfer to paper towels to drain.

5. Add the fried eggplants and soaked chickpeas to the tomato mixture, and simmer for a few more minutes.

6. Serve hot. Enjoy with pita bread.

ingredients:

3 medium eggplants (1.2kg)

½ tsp plus ½ tbsp salt, divided

¼ cup (60ml) vegetable oil, plus more for spraying and frying eggplant

Several small yellow onions

1 head garlic, peeled and minced

5 medium tomatoes (710g), chopped

2 tbsp tomato paste

½ tsp black pepper

½ tsp **Lebanese 7 Spices (page 261)**

1 medium red chili pepper (20g), chopped

1½ cups (530g) cooked chickpeas

note:

The eggplants can be baked instead of fried if you prefer. Preheat the oven to 400°F (200°C). Spray or brush the eggplant cubes with vegetable oil, spread in an even layer on a baking sheet lined with parchment paper and sprayed with a bit of oil, and bake for between 25 and 32 minutes, flipping over halfway through the cook time.

Mujaddara Hamra
LENTILS WITH BULGUR

PREP TIME: **10 MINUTES** + 10 minutes (resting)	COOK TIME: **30 MINUTES**	TOTAL TIME: **40 MINUTES** + resting

SERVES: 8
VEGAN

Mujaddara Hamra is a popular Lebanese picnic food. This tasty, comforting dish needs no seasoning yet has exceptional flavor. We serve it with fresh veggies or salad and Laban Ayran (Salted Yogurt Drink; page 219).

ingredients:

2 cups (420g) dried red lentils, rinsed and any small stones discarded

6 cups (1.4 liters) water, divided

1 tbsp salt

1 cup (250ml) vegetable oil

3 small red onions (316g), finely chopped

1¼ cups (278g) coarse **Bulgur Wheat (Crushed Wheat; page 242)**

⅔ cup (150ml) extra-virgin olive oil

1. In a large pot over medium heat, combine the lentils, 4 cups (1 liter) water, and salt. Bring to a boil, and cook, uncovered, for 25 minutes.

2. Meanwhile, in a large pan over medium-low heat, heat the vegetable oil. Add the onions, and fry, stirring continuously, for 10 minutes or until the onions become very dark brown. This is critical for the success of the dish because the final brownish color and slightly bitter taste depends on this step.

3. Drain and discard the excess oil from the onions, and carefully add the remaining 2 cups (500ml) water to the pan. Increase the heat to medium-high, and bring to a boil. Reduce the heat to low, and simmer for 7 minutes or until the onions are well cooked.

4. Carefully sieve the mixture into a bowl. The fried onions will mostly disintegrate in the water and pass through the sieve. Whatever is left, press with a spatula or the back of a spoon to push through the sieve.

5. Pour the fried onion water over the cooked lentils in the pot. Add the Bulgur Wheat, set over medium-high heat, and bring to a boil. Reduce the heat to very low, and simmer, uncovered and stirring occasionally, for 10 minutes.

6. Turn off the heat, add the olive oil, and stir. Let the dish rest for at least 10 minutes before serving.

7. Serve hot. Enjoy with pita bread, pickles, tomatoes, onion, radishes, salad, or Laban Ayran (Salted Yogurt Drink; page 219).

Moudardara

LENTILS WITH RICE & CARAMELIZED ONIONS

PREP TIME: **5 MINUTES**	COOK TIME: **30 MINUTES**	TOTAL TIME: **35 MINUTES**

SERVES: 4

VEGAN

GLUTEN FREE

This lentil, rice, and caramelized onion dish is packed with sweet and earthy flavors.

ingredients:

1 cup (240g) dried brown lentils, rinsed and any small stones discarded

½ cup (100g) long-grain rice, washed well, rinsed, and drained

3½ cups (875ml) water

1 tsp salt

½ cup (125ml) vegetable oil

2 medium red onions (240g), thinly sliced

1. In a large pot over medium-high heat, combine the lentils, rice, water, and salt. Bring to a boil, reduce the heat to medium-low, and cook, uncovered, for 20 minutes.

2. Meanwhile, in a large skillet over high heat, heat the oil. Add the onions, and fry, stirring occasionally, for 10 minutes or until the onions are caramelized in color. Remove the onions from the oil, set aside, and reserve the oil.

3. After 20 minutes, check one lentil for doneness. It should be just al dente. If it's nearly done, add the oil from the fried onions to the lentils. Stir the lentils, cover, reduce the heat to low, and cook for 10 more minutes.

4. Serve hot with the fried onions on top of the rice and lentil mixture. Enjoy with a salad or yogurt.

Kamounit Banadoura

TOMATOES WITH BULGUR

PREP TIME: **15 MINUTES**	COOK TIME: **NONE**	TOTAL TIME: **15 MINUTES**

SERVES: 4
VEGAN

This summer vegetable recipe reminds me of home and transports me back to South Lebanon. The Kamouneh (Green Bulgur Mix; page 257) gives this healthy, earthy dish its spice and flavor.

ingredients:

½ cup (80g) fine **Bulgur Wheat (Crushed Wheat; page 242)**

½ cup (37g) **Kamouneh (Green Bulgur Mix; page 257)**

½ tsp salt

½ cup (125ml) water

1 tbsp tomato paste

1 cup (200g) chopped tomatoes

3 green onions (48g), finely chopped

½ cup (15g) fresh flat-leaf parsley leaves, chopped

½ cup (12g) fresh mint leaves, chopped

⅓ cup (125ml) extra-virgin olive oil

TO SERVE:

Extra-virgin olive oil

Pita bread

3 green onions

3 radishes

notes:

It's best to eat Kamounit Banadoura immediately after preparation for the best tangy tomato and herby flavors.

If you prefer your bulgur not have a crunch (which is the traditional way), you can presoak it in water for about 30 minutes and drain it before using.

1. In a large bowl, combine the Bulgur Wheat, Kamouneh, salt, water, and tomato paste, stirring until the tomato paste disappears. Set aside for 10 minutes or until the bulgur absorbs the water and gets softer.

2. Add the tomatoes, chopped green onions, parsley, mint, and olive oil, and mix well.

3. Serve immediately on a shallow plate with a good drizzle of olive oil on the top and pita bread, green onions, and radishes on the side.

Fatteh Batenjen

EGGPLANT FATTEH

<table>
<tr><td>PREP TIME: 10 MINUTES
+ 1 hour (sweating)</td><td>COOK TIME: 10 MINUTES</td><td>TOTAL TIME: 20 MINUTES
+ sweating</td></tr>
</table>

SERVES: 1

Fattet Batenjen can be made using a variety of methods. This basic recipe is quick and calls for easy-to-find ingredients. It's seasonal any time of the year—and always delicious.

ingredients:

1 medium eggplant (250g)

1 tsp salt, divided

Vegetable oil, for frying

1 cup (230g) plain full-fat yogurt

½ tsp dried mint

1 large clove garlic, grated

1 tbsp pine nuts

1½ tbsp melted butter or ghee

1 cup (60g) crispy pita chips

1½ cups (270g) cooked chickpeas, or canned

1 tbsp **Tahini (Sesame Paste; page 250)**

¼ tsp black pepper

Fresh flat-leaf parsley leaves

Handful of pomegranate seeds (optional)

notes:

Salting the eggplant helps it release, or "sweat," some of its liquid and bitterness. It also makes it less likely to absorb oil as it fries.

To make the crispy pita chips, cut 1 large or 2 small pitas into small, single-layer squares and bake at 400°F (200°C) for 7 minutes or until golden and crispy.

To bake the eggplant instead of frying it, preheat the oven to 400°F (200°C). Spray or brush the eggplant cubes with vegetable oil, spread in an even layer on a baking sheet lined with parchment paper and sprayed with a bit of oil, and bake for 25 to 32 minutes, flipping over halfway through.

For a looser yogurt sauce, add 3 or 4 tablespoons water in step 3.

1. Cut the eggplant into 1- or 2-inch (2.5–5cm) cubes all about the same size so they'll cook evenly. Rub the cubes with ½ teaspoon salt, place them in a strainer on top of a large bowl, and set aside for 1 hour to "sweat."

2. In a large, deep saucepan over high heat, heat some oil. Add the eggplant cubes in small batches, and fry for 2 to 4 minutes, turning often, until golden and crispy. Transfer to paper towels to drain.

3. In a small bowl, mix the yogurt with the mint, garlic, and the remaining ½ teaspoon salt.

4. In a small saucepan over medium-high heat, pan-fry the pine nuts in the butter for 2 or 3 minutes.

5. To assemble the fattet, in a large bowl, first place the pita chips in the bottom of the bowl and then cover with the chickpeas. Add the yogurt mixture, followed by the eggplant cubes. Sprinkle on the pine nuts, and drizzle the Tahini over all. Season with black pepper, and add a few parsley leaves. Top with pomegranate seeds (if using), and serve.

Kibbet Batata

POTATO KIBBEH

| PREP TIME: **5 MINUTES** | COOK TIME: **50 MINUTES** | TOTAL TIME: **55 MINUTES** |

SERVES: 3
VEGAN

Warm up cold days with this earthy-flavored potato dish you can make with just a few ingredients. It's spiced with my favorite Kamouneh mix and tastes amazing.

ingredients:

3 medium russet potatoes (516g), whole and unpeeled

4 cups (1 liter) water, divided

¼ cup (37g) fine **Bulgur Wheat (Crushed Wheat; page 242)**

½ cup (48g) **Kamouneh (Green Bulgur Mix; page 257)**

½ tsp salt

4 tbsp extra-virgin olive oil, divided

3 radishes

3 green onions

storage:

Although you can store Kibbet Batata in an airtight container in the refrigerator for up to 3 days, it's better to eat it immediately. Storing it affects the flavor.

1. In a large pot over medium-high heat, bring the potatoes and water to a boil. Cook for about 45 to 50 minutes or until the potatoes are well done and pierce easily with a fork. Peel the potatoes, place in a bowl, and mash.

2. Add the Bulgur Wheat, Kamouneh, salt, and 2 tablespoons olive oil. Mix everything together, preferably by hand, until well combined.

3. Serve immediately in a shallow dish. Using a spoon, make slits in the top to pool the oil. Drizzle on the remaining 2 tablespoons olive oil, and serve with radishes and green onions.

Baklet Banadoura

BULGUR & TOMATO

PREP TIME: **5 MINUTES**   COOK TIME: **25 MINUTES**   TOTAL TIME: **30 MINUTES**

SERVES: 2–3

VEGAN

This bulgur and rice recipe is simple but very tasty—and a great way to put leftover tomatoes to good use. It's often served with yogurt.

1. In a large saucepan over medium-high heat, heat the oil. Add the onion, and fry for 5 minutes or until translucent.

2. Add the vermicelli, and stir to incorporate.

3. Add the tomatoes, salt, pepper, cinnamon, and tomato paste, and stir-fry for 2 or 3 minutes.

4. Add the water and Bulgur Wheat. Reduce the heat to low, cover, and simmer for 10 to 15 minutes.

5. Serve hot. Enjoy with a salad or plain yogurt or Laban Ayran (Salted Yogurt Drink; page 219).

ingredients:

½ cup (125ml) olive oil

1 small yellow onion (111g), chopped

⅓ cup (35g) vermicelli noodles

2 medium tomatoes (200g), chopped

1 tsp salt

¼ tsp black pepper

1 tsp ground cinnamon

2 tbsp tomato paste

3 cups (750ml) water

1 cup (174g) coarse **Bulgur Wheat (Crushed Wheat; page 242)**

Desserts & Beverages

Baklawa

BAKLAVA

PREP TIME: **30 MINUTES**	COOK TIME: **1 HOUR**	TOTAL TIME: **1 HOUR 30 MINUTES**
+ 6 hours (absorbing)		+ absorbing

MAKES: about 30 pieces

This classic Middle Eastern dessert looks difficult to make, but it's actually quite easy to put together—just a lot of layers. Baklava is always popular at celebrations and holidays or as a gift for someone who loves sweets.

ingredients:

14 oz (400g) phyllo dough (24 or more sheets)

1¼ cups (290g) butter, melted

2½ cups (320g) pistachios, shelled and crushed in a food processor to a chunky-crumb consistency, plus more for garnish

1½ cups (300ml) **Kater** (Sugar Syrup; page 252) or honey

storage:

Store in an airtight container at room temperature for up to 1 week or in the refrigerator for up to 2 or 3 weeks; or freeze, tightly wrapped in small batches, for up to 3 months.

note:

If you don't have a large 15-inch (37.5cm) round baking pan like the one shown, you can use a 9×13-inch (23×33cm) pan.

variations:

Instead of pistachios, you can use the same amount of walnuts, almonds, or even a combination of nuts.

For even more flavor, you can infuse the syrup. Add 2 cardamom pods, lightly crushed, to the Kater as it cooks. When you're ready to pour it over the hot baklava, remove from the heat, strain the mixture to remove the cardamom, and add ½ teaspoon Maa al Ward (Rose Water; page 244).

1. Preheat the oven to 325°F (165°C), fan assisted.

2. Cut the layered phyllo dough to fit your pan. Keep the cut phyllo under a damp towel to prevent it from drying.

3. Brush some melted butter on the bottom of the baking pan. Add the first layer of phyllo, and butter it lightly. Repeat with 11 more layers of phyllo and butter, for 12 layers total. Add a layer of pistachios and then repeat with 12 more layers of buttered phyllo. Butter the top layer, too.

4. Using a sharp knife, cut the baklava into diamonds or rectangles. Note this happens before it's baked.

5. Bake on the middle oven rack for about 1 hour, checking on it after 30 minutes, until the pastry is golden brown and crisp. If the top is browning too quickly, cover the pan with foil or place a baking sheet on the top rack to reduce the browning slightly.

6. Remove the baklava from the oven, and immediately pour the Kater over the pastry. Set aside to cool and absorb the syrup for 6 hours or overnight before garnishing with more crushed pistachios, if you like, and serving.

Baklawet Ash l Bolbol

BIRD'S NEST BAKLAVA

PREP TIME: **25 MINUTES**	COOK TIME: **15 MINUTES**	TOTAL TIME: **40 MINUTES**

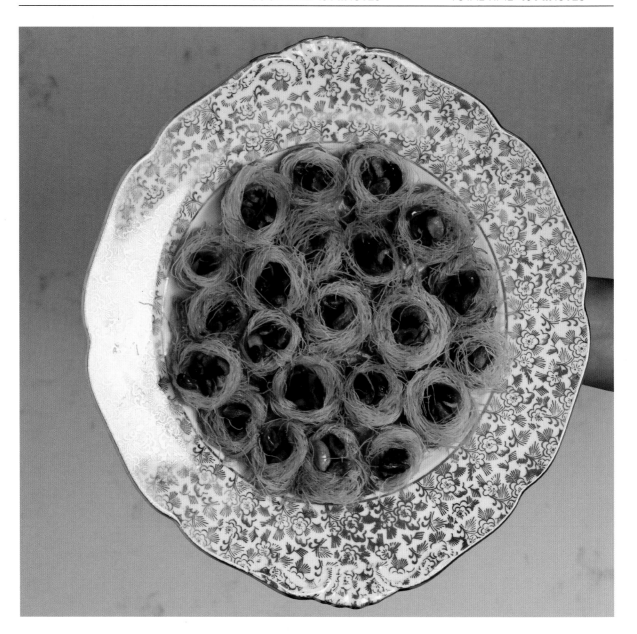

MAKES: 5 to 55 nests

Bird's nests are the easiest crunchy sweets to make. The crunch factor of the nests gives your mouth a slightly surprising sensation as you bite into them, and the sweet gives your taste buds something delightful, too.

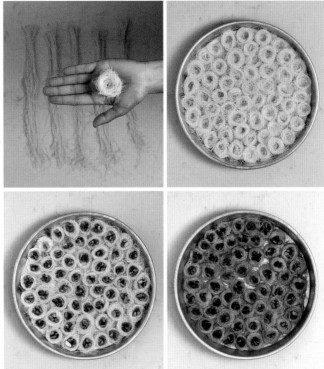

ingredients:

14.5 oz (415g) shredded phyllo dough or kataifi dough

½ cup (100g) unsalted butter, melted

1 cup (106g) pistachios, shelled

⅓ cup (125ml) **Kater (Sugar Syrup; page 252)** or honey

1. Preheat the oven to 350°F (180°C).

2. Place the shredded phyllo dough in a large bowl, and pour the melted butter over the top. Using your hands, gently massage the dough to coat it in the butter. Alternatively, the butter can be poured over the nests right before baking, but I prefer buttering the dough before forming the nests.

3. Cut the buttered dough into strands 12 inches (30cm) long. Gather a small bundle of the dough and shape it into a small nest by rolling the strands of dough around 1 or 2 fingers and twisting them to create the nest. I use 1 finger for the mini nests and 2 fingers for the medium nests.

4. Place the nests on a baking sheet, and sprinkle some pistachios in the center of each nest.

5. Bake at 350°F (180°C) for 15 minutes. Keep an eye on the nests because they can burn quickly.

6. Remove from the oven, transfer to a plate, drizzle the Kater over the top, and serve hot.

Osmalieh

ROASTED SHREDDED PHYLLO WITH ASHTA CREAM

PREP TIME: **5 MINUTES** COOK TIME: **20 MINUTES** TOTAL TIME: **25 MINUTES**

SERVES: 8

This irresistible dessert, commonly prepared during Ramadan, is considered the perfect end to an Iftar meal.

ingredients:

3 cups (750ml) lukewarm water
(105°F–110°F/40°C–43°C)

2 cups (285g) all-purpose flour

1 cup (150g) fine semolina flour

1 tbsp sugar

½ tbsp ground mahlab

2 tbsp powdered milk

1 tsp dry yeast

1 tbsp baking powder, dissolved
in ½ cup (125ml) lukewarm water

Vegetable oil, for frying (optional)
and deep-frying

1 lb (500g) **Kashta (Lebanese Clotted
Cream; page 247)**

3 tbsp ground pistachios (optional)

1 cup (250ml) **Kater (Sugar Syrup;
page 252)**

note:

Watch that you don't overblend in step 2.
If you do, the batter will deflate and your
pancakes won't rise enough. If you do
overblend, let the batter rest again for
15 minutes.

1. In a blender, add the water, all-purpose flour, semolina flour, sugar, mahlab, powdered milk, and yeast. Blend well, and set aside to rest for 15 minutes.

2. Add the dissolved baking powder mixture to the rested batter, and blend for 5 seconds.

3. Heat a nonstick skillet or griddle greased with vegetable oil (if using) over medium heat. When hot, add about 2 tablespoons batter. Lots of bubbles will form on the pancake. When the bubbles form and dry, remove the pancake from the heat. Do not flip to cook the other side. Instead, transfer to a towel, bubbly side up, to dry. As you cook the rest, don't stack the pancakes directly on top of each other. Do keep them covered with a towel.

4. To the center of each pancake, bubbly side up, add about 1 tablespoon Kashta. Fold the pancake in half, and pinch the sides firmly with your fingertips to seal. Pinch the sides together halfway up for a cone qatayef, or continue pinching until fully sealed and then deep-fry the sealed qatayef for 2 minutes or until golden and crisp.

5. Dip in pistachios (if using), arrange on a platter, drizzle with Kater, and serve.

Kunafa bil Jibn

CHEESE KUNAFA

PREP TIME: **15 MINUTES**	COOK TIME: **25 MINUTES**	TOTAL TIME: **40 MINUTES**

MAKES: 3 cups (333g), or
1 (10-inch/25.5cm) round Kunafa

With its sweet, crispy, flaky crust and tangy, stretchy cheese filling, Kunafa is a popular Lebanese sweet. It's best served warm in kaak bread (Lebanese pocket bread) as a breakfast sandwich with a light drizzle of sweet syrup.

ingredients:

Ghee

CRUST:

2 cups (250g) fine semolina flour

2 cups (250g) all-purpose flour

1 tsp baking powder

2 tbsp powdered milk

1 tsp ground mahlab (optional)

1¼ cups (310ml) water

1 tbsp **Maa al Ward (Rose Water; page 244)**

1 tbsp orange blossom water (optional)

¼ cup (60ml) **Kater (Sugar Syrup; page 252)**

¾ cup (150g) melted ghee

notes:

Preparing the kunafa flour and crust are the most important steps in making Kunafa. I usually make a large amount of flour and freeze it in an airtight container for up to 6 months. This recipe yields about 7¼ cups (800g) sifted kunafa flour; 3 cups (333g) are needed to make a medium-size kunafa that's about 10 inches (25.5cm) in diameter.

Using a nonstick baking pan and coating it well with ghee are crucial so the kunafa will come out nicely later and not stick or crack.

PREPARE THE CRUST:

1. Preheat the oven to 350°F (180°C). Grease a nonstick baking sheet with ghee.

2. In a large bowl, whisk together the flours, baking powder, powdered milk, mahlab (if using), water, Maa al Ward, blossom water, Kater, and melted ghee. Continue mixing with your hands to get a firm dough.

3. Spread the dough evenly on the prepared baking sheet, and dimple it all over with your fingertips. Bake for 20 minutes.

4. Remove the crust from the oven, and set aside on a rack to cool for 10 minutes before breaking into pieces.

5. In a food processor, finely grind the crust pieces. Using a mesh strainer, sift the ground crust to ensure no lumps remain and to get a fine flour.

6. Brush the bottom of a nonstick 9- or 10-inch (23–25.5cm) round baking pan well with 2 tablespoons ghee, and evenly spread 3 cups (333g) sifted kunafa flour in the pan. Using your hands, press down all over the flour to be sure you have a flat layer for the crust. Really press well for 3 or 4 minutes to ensure it's very firm so the crust won't collapse when it's flipped later.

CHEESE:

¾ cup (90g) shredded mozzarella

¾ cup (90g) shredded Akkawi cheese, soaked for at least 2 hours to remove the salt and drained very well

1 cup (250ml) warm **Kater (Sugar Syrup; page 252)**

Ground pistachios

storage:

Store in an airtight container in the refrigerator for up to 2 days, or freeze for up to 3 months.

notes:

Soaking the Akkawi cheese removes the salt. Be sure to drain it well before shredding so it's as dry as you can get it.

To reheat the prepared kunafa, place the serving platter over a simmering water bath for 30 minutes. Or you can place it in an oven-safe pan, cover with foil, and reheat in a 350°F (180°C) oven for 10 to 15 minutes.

PREPARE THE CHEESE AND COOK THE KUNAFA:

1. In a small bowl, combine the shredded mozzarella and the soaked, drained, and shredded Akkawi cheese. (Be sure the latter is dry.)

2. Spread the cheeses evenly over the crust, leaving a clean, cheese-free area around the edge so the cheese doesn't stick to the baking pan.

3. Sprinkle a scant ½ cup (45g) kunafa flour over the cheeses to absorb any liquid that may come out of them. This will ensure that the crust doesn't get soggy.

4. Place the baking pan on the stovetop, on the side of a burner set at the lowest heat possible—as low as your stove gets. Avoid putting it directly over the center of the burner so the kunafa won't burn. Cook, rotating the pan every 30 seconds so the crust cooks evenly, for 5 minutes or until you see the edges turn golden.

5. Remove the baking pan from the heat. Invert a plate a little larger than the baking pan on top of the pan, and, wearing oven mitts, flip over the baking pan and plate together. Tap the baking pan gently to release the golden kunafa onto the plate.

6. Pour warm Kater over the top, garnish with ground pistachios, and serve immediately.

Ma'amoul

NUT & DATE FILLED PASTRIES

PREP TIME: **30 MINUTES** + overnight (resting)	COOK TIME: **25 MINUTES**	TOTAL TIME: **55 MINUTES** + resting

MAKES: 15 to 20 cookies

A nut- or date-filled Lebanese cookie usually made during religious holidays, Ma'amoul is extremely rich and delectable. It both crunches and melts in your mouth.

ingredients:

PISTACHIO FILLING PASTE
(makes 5–7 cookies):

½ cup (125g) pistachios, shelled

½ tsp ground cardamom

1 tbsp **Kater (Sugar Syrup; page 252)**

WALNUT FILLING PASTE
(makes 5–7 cookies):

½ cup (120g) walnuts

⅛ tsp ground cinnamon

1 tbsp **Kater (Sugar Syrup; page 252)**

DATE FILLING PASTE
(makes 5–7 cookies):

1 cup (175g) soft Medjool dates, pitted

1½ tbsp melted butter or neutral oil

note:

You'll need one or more ma'amoul molds to shape these cookies. They're available online.

1. Prepare the pistachio filling paste. In a food processor or a blender, roughly chop the pistachios. Add the cardamom and Kater, and blitz again to incorporate. Scoop about 1½ tablespoons of the mixture, and shape into a ball. Repeat with the rest of the mixture. Set aside in an airtight container until ready to use.

2. Prepare the walnut filling paste. In a food processor or a blender, roughly chop the walnuts. Add the cinnamon and Kater, and blitz again to incorporate. Scoop about 1½ tablespoons of the mixture, and shape into a ball. Repeat with the rest of the mixture. Set aside in an airtight container until ready to use.

3. Prepare the date filling paste. In a food processor or blender, roughly chop the dates. Add the butter, and blitz again to incorporate. Scoop about 1½ tablespoons of the mixture, and shape into a ball. Repeat with the rest of the mixture. Refrigerate in an airtight container until ready to use.

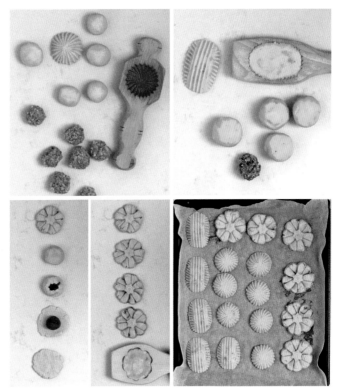

COOKIE DOUGH
(makes 15–20 cookies):

1 cup (120g) all-purpose flour

4 cups (237g) fine semolina flour

2 cups (164g) coarse semolina flour

2 cups (480g) ghee or butter, melted

2½ tsp kaak spice, or ½ tsp each ground fennel seeds, ground cardamom, ground cinnamon, ground ginger, and ground anise

2 tbsp milk powder

¼ cup (112g) powdered sugar

1 tbsp water, plus more if needed

storage:

Store the cooled Ma'amoul in an airtight container at room temperature for up to 1 week.

4. Prepare the cookie dough. Into a large bowl, sift the all-purpose and fine semolina flours. Add the coarse semolina flour and ghee, and mix with your hands. Cover and set aside overnight. Every few hours, mix the dough with your hands or a spatula.

5. The next day, preheat the oven to 350°F (175°C). Line a baking sheet with parchment paper.

6. Add the kaak spice, milk powder, and powdered sugar to the dough. Add water gradually, starting with 1 tablespoon and adding more if needed, until the dough holds together.

7. Scoop about 2 tablespoons of dough, form into a ball, and press in the center to create a well. Stuff with 1 pistachio, walnut, or date paste filling ball. Carefully close the dough over the filling and place in the ma'amoul mold. Press firmly but gently so the dough takes the shape of the mold and all its crevices. Remove the cookie by flipping over the mold and hitting it on a surface. Repeat with the remaining dough and filling.

8. Place the cookies on the baking sheet, leaving some space between them. Bake for 20 to 25 minutes or until lightly golden. Allow to cool completely before serving.

Sfouf

LEBANESE TURMERIC CAKE

PREP TIME: **10 MINUTES** + 15 minutes (chilling)	COOK TIME: **40 MINUTES**	TOTAL TIME: **50 MINUTES** + chilling

SERVES: 9

An eggless cake spiced with turmeric and cinnamon, Sfouf is golden and moist—the perfect afternoon treat.

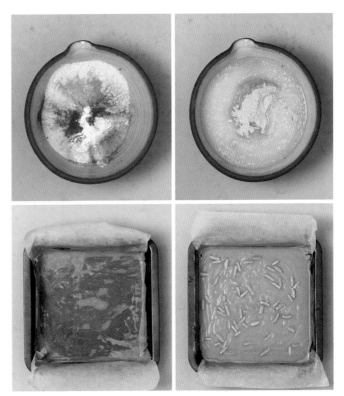

ingredients:

2 tbsp **Tahini (Sesame Paste; page 250)**

1 cup (127g) all-purpose flour

1 cup (146g) coarse semolina flour

1 cup (200g) sugar

1 tsp baking powder

1½ tsp ground turmeric

½ tsp salt

½ tsp ground cinnamon

1 cup (250ml) whole milk

½ cup (125ml) vegetable oil

½ cup (80g) melted butter or ghee

2 tbsp raw pine nuts

storage:

Store in an airtight container at room
temperature for up to 5 to 7 days, or
in the refrigerator for up to 10 days,
or freeze for up to 3 months.

1. Preheat the oven to 355°F (180°C). Grease a 9×9-inch (23×23cm) baking pan with Tahini, and line it with parchment paper.

2. In a large bowl, whisk the all-purpose flour, semolina flour, sugar, baking powder, turmeric, salt, and cinnamon.

3. Add the milk, vegetable oil, and butter, and mix well.

4. Pour the sfouf mixture into the prepared baking pan, and sprinkle the pine nuts over the top.

5. Bake on the middle oven rack for 40 minutes.

6. Remove from the oven, and let cool for 15 minutes before slicing into squares or diamonds and serving.

Sanioura/Ghraybeh

BUTTER COOKIES

PREP TIME: **15 MINUTES** + 1 hour 10 minutes (cooling & resting)	COOK TIME: **15 MINUTES**	TOTAL TIME: **30 MINUTES** + cooling & resting

MAKES: 15–20 cookies

These Levantine cookies are perfect at tea time—or any time! Every bite is buttery, crisp, and scrumptious.

ingredients:

½ cup (104g) butter, softened, or room-temperature ghee

¼ cup (40g) powdered sugar

1½ cups (184g) all-purpose flour

⅛ tsp salt

1 tsp orange blossom water

15–20 pistachios (10g)

storage:

Store in an airtight container at room temperature for up to 1 week.

1. In a large bowl, or the bowl of a stand mixer, whisk together the butter and powdered sugar for 4 to 7 minutes or until the mixture is fluffy and pale.

2. Sift in the all-purpose flour, and add the salt and orange blossom water. Mix using a spatula, wooden spoon, or the stand mixer paddle attachment for 3 to 5 minutes or until the dough is smooth and uniform. Shape the dough into a ball, cover tightly with plastic wrap, and refrigerate for 1 hour.

3. Preheat the oven to 320°F (160°C), fan assisted. Line a baking sheet with parchment paper. Remove the dough from the refrigerator, and let it rest for 10 minutes at room temperature.

4. Cut off about 1 tablespoon of dough, and shape it into a small diamond. Press the dough onto the prepared baking sheet into a cookie ½ inch (1.25cm) thick, and lightly press a pistachio in the center. Repeat with the remaining dough for 15 to 20 cookies. Space them out on the baking sheet so they're not touching.

5. Bake for 15 minutes or until the cookies are cooked through but pale and white, not golden brown. Allow to cool before serving.

Awamat

LEBANESE DOUGHNUT BALLS

PREP TIME: **5 MINUTES**	COOK TIME: **15 MINUTES**	TOTAL TIME: **20 MINUTES**
+ 30 minutes (rising)		+ rising

SERVES: 8
VEGAN

Bring the Middle East to you with these crisp and crunchy Lebanese doughnut balls. They're a sweet end to lunch or a treat with a cup of unsweetened tea.

ingredients:

¾ cup (95g) all-purpose flour

2 tbsp cornstarch

⅛ tsp salt

1 tsp active dry yeast

1 tsp sugar

½ tsp ground mahlab (optional)

½ cup (125ml) lukewarm water
(105°F–110°F/40°C–43°C)

1 tbsp vegetable oil, plus more for
frying

½ cup (125ml) **Kater (Sugar Syrup;
page 252)**

Coarsely ground pistachios (optional)

1. In a large bowl, combine the all-purpose flour, cornstarch, salt, active dry yeast, sugar, and mahlab (if using).

2. Pour the lukewarm water over the dry ingredients, and stir until a dough forms. Set aside to rise for about 30 minutes.

3. In a large frying pan, heat some oil to 375°F (190°C), deep enough to deep-fry the dough balls. Oil your hands with vegetable oil, scoop about 1 tablespoon of dough, and form it into a ball. Carefully place the dough ball in the hot oil. Repeat a few more times so you're frying several dough balls at once without overcrowding the pan. Fry each ball for 2 or 3 minutes or until they're golden brown and float at the surface of the oil. Remove with a slotted spoon, and set on paper towels to absorb any excess oil. Repeat with the rest of the dough.

4. Pour Kater over the awamat while they're still hot, garnish with some ground pistachios (if using), and serve immediately.

Kaak el Eid

HOLIDAY COOKIES

PREP TIME: **15 MINUTES** + 30 minutes (resting)	COOK TIME: **15 MINUTES**	TOTAL TIME: **30 MINUTES** + resting

MAKES: about 15 cookies

These traditional cookies are prepared mostly during religious festivals. Their rich aroma and unique taste will have you reaching for more.

ingredients:

4 cups (506g) all-purpose flour

1 cup (154g) light brown sugar

1 tbsp ground mahlab

1 tbsp baking powder

1 tbsp nigella seeds

1 tbsp ground anise

½ tsp ground cinnamon

½ tsp ground ginger

¼ tsp ground nutmeg

1 cup (250ml) whole milk

1 cup (160g) melted ghee

Vegetable oil

note:

Traditionally, Kaak el Eid get their gorgeous imprint patterns from molds. Kaak molds can be found at Middle Eastern grocery stores and online. Sometimes called wooden molds for Kaak el Abbas, they come in plastic or wood and in a variety of sizes and patterns.

1. In a large bowl, whisk together the all-purpose flour, brown sugar, mahlab, baking powder, nigella seeds, anise, cinnamon, ginger, and nutmeg.

2. Add the milk and melted ghee, and knead until fully incorporated and no dry spots remain. Cover and let the dough rest for 30 minutes.

3. Preheat the oven to 350°F (180°C). Brush a baking sheet with vegetable oil and line with parchment paper.

4. Divide the dough into about 15 small balls. If you have a mold, brush it with vegetable oil, and press a dough ball on it lightly to prevent the dough from sticking. If you don't have a mold, you can flatten and shape the cookies by hand.

5. Place the cookies on the prepared baking sheet about 1 inch (2.5cm) apart. Bake for 15 minutes or until golden.

6. Cool on a rack, and serve.

Avocado Mousse

| PREP TIME: **5 MINUTES** | COOK TIME: **NONE** | TOTAL TIME: **5 MINUTES** |

SERVES: 6
GLUTEN FREE

Avocado Mousse is a unique and scrumptious sweet served at Lebanese cocktail places. It's fluffy and healthy and topped with creamy Kashta and nuts.

ingredients:

4 large ripe avocados (1kg), peeled
and pit removed

3 tbsp honey, plus more for serving

¼ cup (60ml) full-fat milk, plus more
as needed

1 cup (255g) **Kashta (Lebanese
Clotted Cream; page 247)**

2 tbsp soaked pine nuts

2 tbsp blanched almonds

2 tbsp blanched pistachios

Dried edible rose petals

note:

Soak the pine nuts in room-temperature
water for 1 hour before using to soften
them a bit.

1. In a blender or food processor, blend the avocado flesh
   with the honey and milk until completely smooth.

2. Spoon into serving glasses. Add a dollop of Kashta
   on top, and sprinkle with the pine nuts, almonds,
   and pistachios.

3. Drizzle on more honey if you like, garnish with rose
   petals, and serve immediately.

Pistachio Booza

LEBANESE ICE CREAM

PREP TIME: **5 MINUTES** + overnight (freezing)	COOK TIME: **5 MINUTES**	TOTAL TIME: **10 MINUTES** + freezing

SERVES: 10
GLUTEN FREE

Pistachio Booza is the ultimate Lebanese ice cream, distinguished by its intense mastic flavors and extraordinary chewy texture.

ingredients:

3 cups (750ml) full-fat milk

½ cup (53g) cornstarch

3 cups (750ml) heavy cream

2 tsp ground mahlab

½ tsp mastic gum, finely ground

1 cup (200g) sugar

Pinch of salt

1 cup (100g) finely chopped pistachios

note:

You can use a mortar and pestle or an electric spice grinder to grind the mastic gum.

1. In a large pot, whisk a bit of milk and the cornstarch to make a slurry.

2. Whisk in the remaining milk, heavy cream, mahlab, mastic gum, sugar, and salt.

3. Set the pot over medium-low heat, and cook, stirring constantly, for a few minutes until the mixture gets thick and creamy.

4. Turn off the heat just before the mixture starts to boil, and let it cool for a few minutes.

5. Add the pistachios, and stir well.

6. Place the ice cream base in a freezer-safe container, and freeze overnight for best results.

Riz bil Halib

RICE PUDDING

PREP TIME: **5 MINUTES** + 1 hour (cooling)	COOK TIME: **20 MINUTES**	TOTAL TIME: **25 MINUTES** + cooling

SERVES: 6–8

GLUTEN FREE

Riz bil Halib is a traditional Lebanese rice pudding. It's delicious served cold with crushed pistachios on top and drizzled with Kater (Sugar Syrup; page 252).

ingredients:

1 cup (200g) short-grain rice

4 cups (1 liter) water

¼ cup (25g) cornstarch

4¼ cups (1 liter) whole milk

1 cup (250ml) double or heavy cream

⅓ cup (72g) sugar or to taste

¼ tsp mistiki (optional)

1 tsp orange blossom water or **Maa al Ward (Rose Water; page 244)**

TO SERVE:

Ground pistachios

Dried edible rose petals

Ground cinnamon (optional)

Drizzle of honey or **Kater (Sugar Syrup; page 252)** (optional)

1. Rinse the rice several times until the water runs clear. Drain.

2. In a large pan over medium-high heat, combine the rice and water. Bring to a boil, cover, reduce heat to medium-low, and simmer for 10 to 15 minutes or until very well cooked.

3. Meanwhile, in a small bowl, mix the cornstarch with a bit of milk, and stir to dissolve the cornstarch and make a slurry.

4. To the cooked rice, add the cornstarch slurry, the rest of the milk, the cream, the sugar, and the mistiki (if using). Bring to a soft boil over medium heat, and cook, stirring constantly, for 3 or 4 minutes or it becomes thick and creamy. Remove from the heat.

5. Add the orange blossom water, and stir to incorporate.

6. Let the pudding cool slightly and then pour it into serving glasses or small bowls. Allow to cool to room temperature before refrigerating for 1 hour.

7. Serve cold, topped with ground pistachios, rose petals, and cinnamon (if using) and drizzled with honey (if using).

Meghli

SPICED RICE PUDDING

| PREP TIME: **30 MINUTES**
+ 4 hours (soaking/cooling) | COOK TIME: **20 MINUTES** | TOTAL TIME: **50 MINUTES**
+ soaking/cooling |

SERVES: 6
VEGAN
GLUTEN FREE

Meghli is a tasty rice pudding served after the birth of a new baby to express happiness and pride. When topped with soaked nuts and shredded coconut, it doesn't get much better.

ingredients:

1 cup (155g) rice flour

1 cup (200g) sugar

½ tbsp ground cinnamon

2 tbsp ground caraway

½ tbsp ground anise

⅛ tsp salt

7 cups (1.7 liters) water

TOPPINGS:

1 tbsp blanched pine nuts

1 tbsp pistachios

1 tbsp almonds

1 tbsp walnuts

1 tbsp golden raisins

1 tbsp shredded unsweetened coconut

1 tbsp dried edible rose petals

1. Place the pine nuts, pistachios, almonds, walnuts, and golden raisins in separate small bowls, and fill the bowls with cold or hot water. If using cold water, soak for at least 4 hours or overnight. If using hot water, soak for 30 minutes. Drain.

2. Peel the soaked almonds and pistachios.

3. Meanwhile, in a large pot, combine the rice flour, sugar, cinnamon, caraway, anise, and salt.

4. Add the water to the pot, and mix well to incorporate.

5. Set the pot over medium-low heat, and cook, whisking constantly, for about 20 minutes or until the mixture thickens. Remove from the heat.

6. Pour the pudding into serving glasses or bowls. Allow to cool to room temperature before refrigerating for at least 4 hours.

7. Serve cold, topping each glass with a layer of shredded coconut, and a few of the soaked and peeled nuts, the raisins, and the rose petals.

Morabah al Lakteen

CANDIED PUMPKIN

PREP TIME: **15 MINUTES** + 5 hours (soaking)	COOK TIME: **4 HOURS**	TOTAL TIME: **4 HOURS 15 MINUTES** + soaking

SERVES: 15

VEGAN

GLUTEN FREE

The sweet pumpkin flavors of autumn are captured in this unique candied pumpkin dessert.

ingredients:

½ cup (60g) pickling lime

2 lb (1kg) pumpkin, washed, peeled, and chopped into 1-in (2.5cm) cubes

4¾ cups (1kg) sugar

2 qt (2 liters) water

½ cup (125ml) freshly squeezed lemon juice

storage:

Store in a sterilized, airtight container in the refrigerator for up to 3 months.

1. In a large bowl, dissolve the pickling lime in plenty of water. Set aside for 10 to 15 minutes.

2. Add the pumpkin cubes to the pickling lime water, and set aside to soak for 5 or 6 hours.

3. Thoroughly rinse the pickling lime off the pumpkin cubes until the pieces are completely clean of lime. This should take 5 or 6 rinses.

4. Place the washed pumpkin in a large saucepan, add the sugar and 2 quarts (2 liters) water, and bring to a boil over medium-high heat, skimming off any foam that rises to the top. Reduce the heat to medium-low, and simmer for 3 or 4 hours. The mixture will thicken as it cooks. It's ready when the sauce sticks to the back of a spoon.

5. Add the lemon juice, stir to incorporate, and remove from the heat.

6. Let cool and then store in a clean, sterilized container. Enjoy as is, or blend into a smooth purée.

Tin M'aqqad

FIG CONSERVE

| PREP TIME: **5 MINUTES** | COOK TIME: **45 MINUTES** | TOTAL TIME: **50 MINUTES** |

MAKES: about 3 cups (1kg) or 2 medium canning jars

VEGAN

GLUTEN FREE

You'll love the earthy Middle Eastern flavors and the crunchiness of the fig seeds in this tasty fig jam. It's usually served as a spread on toast or pita bread, and it pairs perfectly with Akkawi cheese.

ingredients:

2 cups (328g) dried figs

Water

1 cup (200g) sugar or to taste

Juice of ½ medium lemon

¼ tsp ground mistiki

½ tbsp ground anise

1 tbsp orange blossom water

1½ cups (170g) walnuts, halved

3 tbsp sesame seeds

notes:

If you want, you can cut the figs in half or quarters before cooking. This is the traditional Lebanese way.

Toast the walnuts and sesame seeds for richer flavor if you like. In a large dry (no oil) pan over medium heat, toast the walnuts and sesame seeds separately, stirring constantly, for 2 or 3 minutes or until fragrant.

storage:

Store in clean, sterilized jars in the refrigerator for up to 2 months. It will last up to 1 year if processed by canning in a hot water bath.

1. In a large skillet over medium-high heat, add the dried figs and just enough water to cover. Bring to a soft boil, reduce the heat to low, and simmer, stirring occasionally, for 30 to 40 minutes or until the figs have softened and the liquid has reduced.

2. When the figs are soft, add the sugar, lemon juice, mistiki, anise, and orange blossom water. Continue to simmer for 10 to 15 minutes or until the mixture becomes thick.

3. Add the walnuts and sesame seeds, and stir to incorporate.

4. Remove from the heat, and set aside to cool to room temperature.

5. Pour into clean, sterilized jars; wipe the rims clean; and add the lids.

Fruit Cocktail

PREP TIME: **15 MINUTES**	COOK TIME: **NONE**	TOTAL TIME: **15 MINUTES**

SERVES: 8

GLUTEN FREE

ingredients:

1 cup (125g) chopped strawberries

1 cup (150g) chopped kiwi

1 cup (165g) chopped mango

1 cup (225g) chopped pineapple

1 cup (200g) chopped peaches

1 cup (250ml) strawberry juice

1 cup (240g) mango purée

1 cup (255g) **Kashta (Lebanese Clotted Cream; page 247)**

1 tbsp peeled, blanched almonds

1 tbsp blanched pistachios

1 tbsp blanched pine nuts

8 tbsp honey, divided

notes:

For a creamier consistency, you can use a strawberry milkshake instead of the strawberry juice.

This healthy cocktail is always in season. Its bright flavors and fresh, fruity ingredients are topped with clotted cream and blanched nuts.

1. Evenly divide the strawberry, kiwi, mango, pineapple, and peach chunks among the serving cups.

2. Pour in the strawberry juice and mango purée until the cups are ¾ full.

3. Top each cup with 2 tablespoons Kashta, garnish with about 1 teaspoon blanched nuts, and drizzle with 1 tablespoon honey. Serve chilled. (If the fruits, mango purée, and strawberry juice are cold, there's no need to refrigerate; otherwise, refrigerate for at least 2 hours before serving.)

Rose Lemonade

MAKES: 6 cups (1.4 liters)

VEGAN

GLUTEN FREE

ingredients:

½ cup (62g) fresh raspberries or strawberries

3 cups (750ml) water

1 cup (250ml) **Kater (Sugar Syrup; page 252)**

1 cup (250ml) freshly squeezed lemon juice (5–6 lemons)

½ tbsp **Maa al Ward (Rose Water; page 244)**

Lemon slices

Ice cubes

storage:

Store covered and without the ice cubes in the refrigerator for up to 3 or 4 days.

An easy, healthy drink with a distinctive twist, Rose Lemonade is sweet, tart, and refreshing.

1. Muddle the raspberries into a purée.

2. In a large pitcher, combine the water, Kater, lemon juice, muddled raspberries, and Maa al Ward.

3. Serve immediately with lemon slices and lots of ice cubes.

note:

If you're not serving it right away, don't add the ice. As it melts, it'll water down the whole pitcher.

Laymonada
MINT LEMONADE

PREP TIME: **5 MINUTES**	COOK TIME: **NONE**	TOTAL TIME: **5 MINUTES**

MAKES: 6 cups (1.4 liters)

VEGAN

GLUTEN FREE

ingredients:

1 cup (30g) fresh mint leaves, plus more for garnish

1 cup (250ml) freshly squeezed lemon juice (5–6 lemons)

1 cup (250ml) **Kater (Sugar Syrup; page 252)**

3 cups (750ml) water

Lemon slices

Ice cubes

storage:

Store covered and without the ice cubes in the refrigerator for up to 3 or 4 days.

note:

If you're not serving it right away, don't add the ice. As it melts, it'll water down the whole pitcher.

This fresh, minty lemonade served over ice will cool you down on the warmest of days.

1. In a blender, pulse the mint leaves with a little lemon juice. Alternatively, place the mint leaves and lemon juice in a bowl and use a handheld blender or a muddler to blend.

2. In a large pitcher, combine the lemon juice, Kater, and water with the blended mint.

3. Serve immediately with lemon slices, whole mint leaves, and lots of ice cubes.

Laban Ayran
SALTED YOGURT DRINK

PREP TIME: **2 MINUTES**	COOK TIME: **NONE**	TOTAL TIME: **2 MINUTES**

SERVES: 4

VEGAN (substitute almond or soy yogurt)

GLUTEN FREE

ingredients:

2 cups (490g) plain full-fat yogurt

2 cups (500ml) water

½ tsp salt

1 tsp dried mint

Fresh mint leaves (optional)

Ice cubes

storage:

Store without the ice cubes in a glass bottle in the refrigerator for up to 5 days.

note:

If you're not serving it right away, don't add the ice. As it melts, it'll water down the whole bottle.

Laban Ayran is a refreshing, savory yogurt drink that's quick and easy to make at home.

1. In a large bowl, whisk together the yogurt, water, salt, and dried mint until smooth.

2. Serve immediately, garnished with fresh mint (if using) and lots of ice cubes.

Staples

Vegan Chicken

SEITAN

PREP TIME: **15 MINUTES** + 10 minutes (resting)	COOK TIME: **1 HOUR**	TOTAL TIME: **1 HOUR 15 MINUTES** + resting

MAKES: 2 cups (850g)

VEGAN

Seitan is a great vegan chicken alternative—and a healthier substitute for chicken. You can use it in many of the recipes in this book that call for chicken.

ingredients:

2 cups (256g) vital
wheat gluten

½ cup (69g) chickpea
flour

2 tsp onion powder

2 tsp garlic powder

1 cup (250ml) water

8 cups (1.8 liters)
vegetable broth

notes:

Instead of boiling in broth,
the seitan can be steamed
in parchment paper or
muslin cloth "packets" for
1 hour. The packets prevent
the seitan from expanding
and getting mushy so it
stays firm and meaty.

Try this instead of chicken
in Shorbet Djaj (Chicken
Soup; page 138), Molokhia
bi Aldjaj (Jute Mallow with
Chicken; page 130), Djej
w Batata (Chicken &
Potatoes; page 140), Kabsi
Rice (Rice and Chicken;
page 148), Hareesa
(Chicken Wheat Porridge;
page 132), Moghrabieh
(Lebanese Couscous;
page 134), or Freekeh
with Chicken (Roasted
Green Wheat & Chicken;
page 136).

1. In a large bowl, mix the vital wheat gluten, chickpea flour, onion powder, and garlic powder.

2. Gradually add up to 1 cup (250ml) water, or use up to 1 cup (250ml) vegetable broth. Incorporate the liquid into the dough, and knead for 5 to 10 minutes. The longer you knead, the more developed the dough will be. Cover with a damp kitchen towel, and set aside for about 10 minutes.

3. Meanwhile, in a large saucepan over medium-high heat, bring the vegetable broth to a boil. Reduce the heat to low and let the broth simmer.

4. Chop the dough into 4 or more pieces and add to the simmering broth. Alternatively, you can cube or shred the dough into smaller pieces.

5. Cook, uncovered, for 1 hour. Keep the heat low to avoid boiling the broth.

6. Remove from the heat, and use the seitan hot.

Soy Mince

| PREP TIME: **5 MINUTES** | COOK TIME: **30 MINUTES** | TOTAL TIME: **35 MINUTES** |

MAKES: 2½ cups (400g)

VEGAN

GLUTEN FREE

Try this vegan meat alternative in place of ground beef or lamb. It's full of plant protein, thanks to the tofu, and super flavorful.

ingredients:

15 oz (425g) firm tofu, drained and pressed

¼ cup (60ml) sunflower oil

1½ tbsp soy sauce or tamari

1 tsp smoked paprika

1 tsp onion powder (optional)

1 tsp garlic powder (optional)

2 tbsp nutritional yeast

1 tsp red chili powder (optional)

¼ cup (56g) tomato purée (optional)

storage:

Store in an airtight container in the refrigerator for up to 2 days.

note:

Instead of baking the tofu, you can fry it. In a large skillet over medium heat, heat some oil. Add the seasoned tofu, and cook, stirring frequently, for 15 to 20 minutes, depending on how firm you'd like it.

1. Preheat the oven to 400°F (200°C). Grease a large baking sheet with oil or line with parchment paper.

2. Into a bowl, crumble the tofu. You can do this using a fork, with a potato ricer, or by hand. The pieces don't have to be the same sizes; they can vary to resemble minced meat.

3. In a small bowl, mix the oil, soy sauce, paprika, onion powder (if using), garlic powder (if using), nutritional yeast, chili powder (if using), and tomato purée (if using). Pour over the tofu, gently stir to coat, and spread the seasoned tofu in an even layer on the baking sheet.

4. Bake for 20 to 30 minutes, stirring after 10 to 15 minutes. The exact cook time depends on the size of the tofu pieces and how dry you want it.

5. Use in recipes that call for minced meat.

Braised Beef or Lamb & Broth

PREP TIME: **5 MINUTES** COOK TIME: **1 HOUR 40 MINUTES** TOTAL TIME: **1 HOUR 45 MINUTES**

SERVES: 2 cups (500g) cooked meat & 3 cups (750ml) broth
GLUTEN FREE

Braised beef (mawzat) is a primary Lebanese component in many dishes, especially stews (yakhany). (The same method can be used for lamb.) Braising the meat makes it tender and extra flavorful, and the resulting broth is rich and delicious.

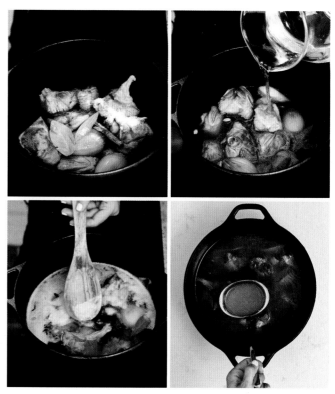

ingredients:

3 tbsp vegetable oil

1 lb (500g) mawzat beef or lamb (shank, short ribs, belly, or chuck; can be bone-in)

5 cardamom pods

1 cinnamon stick

2 bay leaves

2 whole cloves

1 tbsp salt

1–2 small yellow or red onions (250g), peeled

6 cups (1.4 liters) cold water

storage:

Store the cooked meat in an airtight container in the refrigerator for up to 3 days, or freeze for up to 3 months. Store the broth in an airtight container in the refrigerator for up to 1 week, or freeze for up to 4 months.

notes:

To reduce the fat in the broth, you can refrigerate it overnight and discard the layer of fat that solidifies at the top.

There are two methods to prepare the meat. I prefer the method to the right because the beef retains its greasy flavor and is more delicious and juicy. Alternatively, you can use a pressure cooker to sear the meat in the oil and spices. Then add the salt, onions, and water to cover and bring to a boil, skimming off any foam that appears. Reduce the heat to low, cover, and cook for 40 minutes. Turn off the heat, and let the pressure cooker release the steam naturally.

1. In a large pot over medium-high heat, heat the oil. Add the meat, cardamom, cinnamon stick, bay leaves, and cloves, and cook for 4 or 5 minutes or until the beef browns and the spices have released their flavors.

2. Reduce the heat to medium. Add the salt, whole onion(s), and enough cold water to cover the meat. (The amount you need depends on the size of the pot and the size of the meat pieces.)

3. Bring the mixture to a boil, skimming off any foam that appears. Reduce the heat to low, cover, and simmer for at least 1½ hours. (The foam appears only when the mixture is brought to a boil in the first 30 minutes of cooking.)

4. Using a fine-mesh sieve, strain the mixture, reserving the broth. The meat is now tender and flavorful and ready for use in stews and other recipes, and the broth is ready to be used or stored for later.

Market Djaj

CHICKEN BROTH

PREP TIME: **5 MINUTES**	COOK TIME: **1 HOUR**	TOTAL TIME: **1 HOUR 5 MINUTES**

MAKES: 5–6 cups (1.2–1.4 liters)
GLUTEN FREE

Warm and rich chicken broth can be used in many Lebanese dishes, not just stews and soups. It's a very versatile ingredient that brings extra flavor to a recipe.

ingredients:

2 lb (1kg) whole chicken or chicken pieces

1 medium yellow onion (166g), peeled and halved

1 stalk celery (37g), optional

1 medium carrot (60g)

4 cloves garlic

½ in (1.25cm) piece ginger

17 cardamom pods

2 bay leaves

½ tsp whole cloves

½ tsp black peppercorns

1 cinnamon stick

1½ tsp salt

A few sprigs of fresh thyme

storage:

Store in an airtight container in the refrigerator for up to 1 week, or freeze for up to 3 months.

note:

To reduce the fat in the broth, you can refrigerate it overnight and discard the layer of fat that solidifies at the top.

1. Rinse the chicken well under cold water to clean.

2. In a large pot, place the chicken (whole or roughly chopped to fit your pot), onion, celery, carrot, garlic, ginger, cardamom, bay leaves, cloves, peppercorns, cinnamon stick, salt, and thyme.

3. Add enough cold water to cover the chicken. (The amount of water you need depends on the size of the pot and the size of the chicken.)

4. Bring the mixture to a boil over medium heat, skimming off any foam that appears. Reduce the heat to low, cover, and simmer for 1 hour. (The foam appears only when the mixture is brought to a boil in the first 30 minutes of cooking.)

5. Using a fine-mesh sieve, strain the mixture, reserving the broth. The chicken is now cooked and flavorful and ready to use in other recipes, and the broth is ready to be used or stored for later.

Tomato Stew Sauce

| PREP TIME: **5 MINUTES** | COOK TIME: **35 MINUTES** | TOTAL TIME: **40 MINUTES** |

MAKES: 3 cups (600g)
VEGAN
GLUTEN FREE

This classic tomato sauce is popular in Lebanon and used in many recipes and stews (yakhany). It's full of rich, fresh flavor and easy to prepare. Make a double batch so you have a lot on hand.

ingredients:

¼ cup (60ml) vegetable or olive oil

1 medium yellow onion (140g), chopped

2 tbsp tomato paste

¼ tsp black pepper

1 small cinnamon stick

1 tsp salt

¼ tsp red chili powder (optional)

1 small red chili pepper (3g), sliced

1½ cups (330g) chopped tomatoes

½ cup (120ml) water or vegetable stock

storage:

Store in an airtight container in the refrigerator for up to 3 days, or freeze for up to 2 months.

1. In a large skillet over medium heat, heat the oil. Add the onion, and cook for 5 to 8 minutes or until it becomes translucent.

2. Add the tomato paste, black pepper, cinnamon stick, salt, and chili powder (if using). Mix well. Add the sliced fresh chili pepper, and cook for a few more minutes or until it softens.

3. Add the chopped tomatoes and water, and stir to combine. Reduce the heat to medium-low, and simmer for 15 to 25 minutes or until the tomatoes are cooked through and the sauce has reduced to your desired consistency.

4. Remove the cinnamon stick.

5. If you prefer a smooth-textured sauce without chunks, you can process it in the skillet using a handheld blender or transfer the sauce to a food processor to purée.

Al Ajeen

BASIC DOUGH

PREP TIME: **20–25 MINUTES**	COOK TIME: **NONE**	TOTAL TIME: **20–25 MINUTES**
+ 45–60 minutes (rising)		+ rising

MAKES: 800g

VEGAN

This basic bread dough recipe is easy to prepare and works well for Manakish (Breakfast Pies; page 12), Fatayer Sabanekh (Spinach Pies; page 14), Khobz Arabi (Lebanese Pita Bread; page 234), and Lahm bi Ajeen (Mini Meat Pies; page 124).

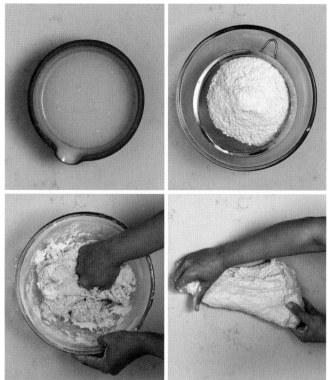

ingredients:

1¼ cups (310ml) lukewarm water (105°F–110°F/ 40°C–43°C)

1 tbsp sugar

1 tsp active dry yeast

1 lb (500g) white bread flour or plain white flour

1½ tsp salt

¼ cup (40g) cornstarch

2 tbsp vegetable oil

Water or olive oil as needed

storage:

Store the prepared dough, wrapped tightly in plastic wrap, in the refrigerator for up to 2 days.

1. In a small bowl, combine the water, sugar, and yeast. Set aside for about 5 to 10 minutes so the yeast can activate. It should froth and become bubbly.

2. In a large bowl, sift together the flour, salt, and cornstarch. When the yeast is active, add it and the oil to the flour mixture. Mix well, first with a spatula to incorporate, and then with your hands, until a sticky dough forms.

3. Knead the dough on a clean surface for 10 minutes or until it becomes smooth and elastic. When poked with a finger, the dough should bounce back; if it doesn't, knead a little longer. Form the kneaded dough into a ball.

4. Place the dough ball in the bowl. Moisten the top of the dough with water or olive oil, cover, and set aside in a warm place to rise for 45 to 60 minutes.

5. After the dough has doubled in size, it's ready to use in your favorite recipe.

Khobz Arabi

LEBANESE PITA BREAD

PREP TIME: **20 MINUTES** + 30 minutes (resting)	COOK TIME: **10 MINUTES**	TOTAL TIME: **30 MINUTES** + resting

MAKES: 10–12

VEGAN

This pita bread is fluffy and light, with the perfect "pocket" shape for filling with your choice of ingredients. No Lebanese meal is complete without it. With the prepared Al Ajeen (Basic Dough; page 232), pitas are simple to make—and taste so much better than store-bought.

ingredients:

1 batch Al Ajeen (Basic Dough; page 232)

storage:

These pitas are best enjoyed fresh but can be kept for up to 5 days at room temperature or frozen for up to 2 months.

1. Divide the rested dough into 10 to 12 equal portions (60–80g each; you can use a scale to be precise). Shape each portion into a ball, working one portion at a time and keeping the rest covered under a towel so they don't dry out.

2. Using a rolling pin and working on a floured surface, roll each ball into a flat circle about ¼ inch (0.5cm) thick. For a perfect circle, you can use a bowl or plate as a template to cut the dough. For a more "rustic" look, leave as is.

3. Place the rolled dough on a floured baking sheet, cover with a slightly damp towel, and let rest for 30 minutes.

4. Meanwhile, place another baking sheet upside down in the oven, and preheat the oven to 480°F (250°C). This will take at least 25 minutes.

5. Carefully place each rolled dough on the inverted baking sheet in the oven for 3 or 4 minutes. The pita bread bakes quickly; it will puff up within minutes and turn a brownish/golden color. As soon as you remove the pitas from the oven, cover them completely with a dry towel to keep them soft and prevent them from crisping. Left uncovered, the pitas will get crispy.

Kaak Abou Arab

LEBANESE STREET BREAD

PREP TIME: **20 MINUTES**
+ 2 hours (rising)

COOK TIME: **30 MINUTES**

TOTAL TIME: **50 MINUTES**
+ rising

MAKES: 6
VEGAN

You'll find this famous Lebanese street bread on vendors' carts on every street in Beirut. It's a good snack for when you're on the go and is often paired with Picón cheese or za'atar and sumac spices.

ingredients:

1½ tbsp dry yeast

3 tbsp sugar

1¾ cups (445ml) lukewarm water (105°F–110°F/ 40°C–43°C)

3½ cups (525g) all-purpose or bread flour

1¾ cups (225g) whole-wheat flour

¼ cup (60ml) extra-virgin olive oil

1½ tbsp salt

1 cup (140g) sesame seeds

storage:

Fresh Kaak Abou Arab is best eaten within 2 or 3 days. Seal it loosely in a paper bag, and store at room temperature. To soften the crust, store it in a plastic bag. Be sure to get as much air out of the bag as possible before sealing.

note:

What to do with the cut-out circle? The mini, ringless Kaak Abou Arab are perfect little puffs. Tuck Kunafa bil Jibn (Cheese Kunafa; page 190) in them, or stuff them with cheese and grill until the cheese melts.

1. In a small bowl, combine the yeast, sugar, and water, and set aside to let the yeast activate.

2. In a large bowl, mix the flours, oil, and salt. Add the yeast mixture, and knead for 7 to 10 minutes or until the dough is soft and smooth. Cover the dough with a damp towel and set aside for 1 hour to double in size.

3. Cut the dough into 6 small equal portions (120g each). Shape each portion into a tight ball, cover with a damp towel, and set aside for 15 minutes.

4. Using a rolling pin and working on a floured surface, roll each ball into a flat circle about ¼ inch (0.5cm) thick. Dip each circle in water, and coat both sides with sesame seeds.

5. Roll once more and then cut out a small circle close to one edge using a cookie cutter or drinking glass. Set aside, covered, for 30 to 45 minutes.

6. In a large dry (no oil) skillet over medium heat, cook each circle, flipping every 10 seconds until a pocket forms, about 3 to 5 minutes. Transfer to a plate, keep warm under a dry towel, and repeat with remaining dough circles.

Markouk
PAPER THIN BREAD

| PREP TIME: **20 MINUTES**
+ 5 hours (rising) | COOK TIME: **1 HOUR 20 MINUTES** | TOTAL TIME: **1 HOUR 40 MINUTES**
+ rising |

MAKES: 80
VEGAN

Markouk is one of the best Lebanese whole-grain breads. It's my first bread memory in the Lebanese mountains; my mother always makes this very thin, wonderfully aromatic flatbread that's fun to prepare, with some practice. It can be served with a variety of meals or as a wrap.

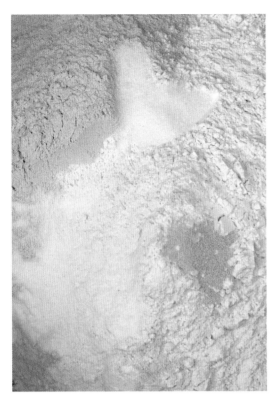

ingredients:

15 cups (1.8kg) whole-wheat flour

26 cups (3.9kg) white flour

½ cup (111g) salt

¼ cup (55g) sugar

1 tsp dry yeast

1¼ gal (4.8 liters) water, plus extra for shaping the dough

Cornmeal

tools:

Round cushion

Saj or wok

1. In a large bowl, sift the whole-wheat and white flours. Add the salt, sugar, and yeast, and mix well. Add the water, and incorporate until a soft dough forms. Knead for 5 to 10 minutes or until you have a smooth, elastic dough.

2. Dipping your hands in water when working with each piece, divide the dough into about 80 even portions. Shape each into a ball, and coat it with cornmeal so the dough balls don't stick together. Place the balls back into the floured bowl, cover with a damp towel, and set aside for at least 5 hours or overnight.

3. Dust your work surface with whole-wheat flour. Take one of the balls, and punch it down onto the surface. Press it lightly to create a large circular shape, dusting with flour so it doesn't stick. Stretch it thin by gently pulling it from one hand to the other. This should be a rather quick, circular motion that allows you to stretch the dough very thinly. We normally use a round cushion to help with this stretching process.

4. Preheat your pan or convex disk; if you're using a wok, invert it. Place the cushion close to your cooking area. Do a final stretch over the pillow to even out the dough; pull the dough gently from all sides until it is paper-thin and becomes quite see-through. Transfer the dough to the pan by flipping over the cushion, and cook for just 1 or 2 minutes. The bread will start browning quickly. It's done when it's slightly hardened.

5. Peel off the markouk, and set it aside on a clean kitchen towel. Wipe away any dough left on the pan, and repeat the process with the rest of the dough, stretching and cooking one ball at a time.

6. When the markouk has cooled, fold it into fours to make a square. Store it in an airtight container or reusable bag in the refrigerator. For freshness, it's best if it's stored in the freezer for up to 1 year.

variation:

For delicious **Za'atar Saj,** spread 2 tablespoons Za'atar paste, made with 2 tablespoons Za'atar (Wild Oregano Mix; page 260) and 3 tablespoons olive oil, on the markouk as it cooks. Remove from the heat, fold in half, and serve.

Riz bi Sh'arieh
RICE WITH VERMICELLI

PREP TIME: **5 MINUTES**	COOK TIME: **25 MINUTES**	TOTAL TIME: **30 MINUTES**

SERVES: 5
VEGAN

ingredients:

2 cups (370g) long-grain rice

2 tbsp vegetable oil

½ cup (30g) broken vermicelli pasta

2½ cups (625ml) water

1 tsp salt

storage:

Store in an airtight container in the refrigerator for up to 3 days, or freeze for 1 or 2 months.

notes:

Rinsing the rice three or four times is important to get fluffy rice.

You can cook the rice in a rice cooker instead. Use a 1-to-1 ratio: 2 cups (370g) rice to 2 cups (500ml) water.

This super simple but flavorful rice is incredibly popular in Middle Eastern and Lebanese cuisine, equally good alongside stews and curries as yogurt. The vermicelli adds nice color, flavor, and texture to the rice.

1. Rinse the rice several times until the water runs clear. Drain.

2. In a large saucepan over medium heat, heat the oil. Add the vermicelli, and stir-fry, stirring constantly, for 1 or 2 minutes or until it turns golden brown. Add the rice, and stir-fry for 1 or 2 minutes. Add the water and salt, and stir. Increase the heat to medium-high, and bring to a boil.

3. Cover the pan, reduce the heat to low, and simmer for 12 minutes or until all the water has been absorbed. Remove from the heat, and set aside, covered, for 10 more minutes.

4. Serve hot.

Bulgur Wheat

CRUSHED WHEAT

PREP TIME: 5 MINUTES
+ 1–2 days (drying)

COOK TIME: 1 HOUR 30 MINUTES

TOTAL TIME: 1 HOUR 35 MINUTES
+ drying

MAKES: 2 pounds (1kg)

VEGAN

A par-boiled, dried, and cracked wheat, bulgur wheat is an essential pantry ingredient in Lebanese cuisine. It's great for making tabbouleh, adding to salads, and using in place of rice or couscous.

ingredients:

2 lb (1kg) wheat berries (durum wheat)

Cold water

storage:

Store in an airtight container
in a cool, dry place for up to 1 year.

note:

To sift the ground bulgur wheat into
different categories—fine, medium,
and coarse—you need at least two
strainers, one fine-mesh and one medium.
You can use a slightly larger one to
separate the coarse and extra-coarse
pieces, too. First use a fine-mesh sieve
to separate out the "floury" consistency
wheat; this can be used as superfine bulgur
for puddings, etc. Then use a sieve with
slightly larger holes to sift again; this
bulgur will be fine bulgur. The remaining
unsifted bulgur will be coarse bulgur.

1. In a large bowl, soak the wheat in enough cold
   water to cover it by 2 inches (5cm). Set aside to
   soak overnight. Drain.

2. In a large saucepan over medium-high heat, combine
   the soaked wheat with enough fresh water to cover
   by at least 1 inch (2.5cm). Bring to a boil, reduce heat
   to medium, and simmer, partially covered, for about
   60 to 90 minutes. The wheat is ready when it breaks
   down when pressed between your finger and thumb.

3. Allow the cooked wheat to dry. You can spread the
   wheat in a single layer on a large tray or multiple trays
   and let it air-dry for 1 or 2 days in a sunny, airy place.
   Or you can spread it on dehydrator trays or baking
   sheets and dehydrate at 100°F (40°C) for 5 or 6 hours
   or until fully dried. You also could spread the wheat on
   baking sheets and dry in the oven at 200°F (95°C) for
   2 or 3 hours until it's dried enough to "crack" easily.

4. Grind and sift the wheat. You can use a blender, grain
   mill, or spice grinder. It's best to grind it in small
   batches. Then sift the mixture to separate the different
   coarsenesses, and store for later use.

Maa al Ward

ROSE WATER

PREP TIME: **5 MINUTES**	COOK TIME: **30 MINUTES**	TOTAL TIME: **35 MINUTES**

MAKES: ⅔ cup (150ml)
VEGAN
GLUTEN FREE

Rose water is used in many Lebanese desserts and drinks but also as a beauty product and scented room mist! It's essential to use only fragrant, organic, chemical- and pesticide-free roses. If you don't start with fragrant roses, your rose water won't be fragrant either.

ingredients:

5 large fragrant organic roses

Water

30 ice cubes

storage:

Store in a cool, dry place or in
the refrigerator for up to 4 months.

note:

Try to find organic damask rose (*Rosa
damascena*) or cabbage rose (*Rosa
centifolia*). Either is beautifully fragrant
and will produce an aromatic rose water.

1. Remove the rose petals from the stems, and carefully rinse them to get rid of any dust or small insects.

2. Set a heatproof bowl in the center of a large pot, and add the rose petals around the outside of the bowl. (The bowl should remain empty at this point; it will collect the condensed rose water later during the cooking process.)

3. Add enough water to cover the petals, set over medium-low heat, and bring to a simmer.

4. Put the lid on the pot, but set it upside down. Add some ice to the inverted lid. This helps with the condensation process.

5. As the ice melts, add more to the lid, repeating the process several times with the remaining ice.

6. After about 30 minutes, the rose water will be ready. It should have condensed into the bowl in the middle of the pot.

7. Carefully remove the bowl—it is hot.

8. Allow the rose water to cool completely and then pour it into a clean glass container.

Kabis

PICKLES

PREP TIME: **10 MINUTES**
+ 48 hours (pickling)

COOK TIME: **5 MINUTES**

TOTAL TIME: **15 MINUTES**
+ pickling

MAKES: 4 jars

VEGAN (omit honey)

GLUTEN FREE

ingredients:

BRINE:

2 cups (500ml) water

2 cups (500ml) apple cider or white vinegar

2 tbsp salt

¼ cup (50g) sugar or honey

PICKLED CUCUMBERS:

2 lb (1kg) small cucumbers

1 tbsp coriander seeds

0.5 oz (15g) fresh dill

2 cloves garlic

PICKLED TURNIPS:

2 lb (1kg) turnips, peeled and chopped

1–2 cloves garlic

1 small beet, peeled and chopped (optional)

PICKLED CHILIES:

2 lb (1kg) chili peppers

2–3 cloves garlic

notes:

Sterilize all the tools and canning jars you're using, and let them dry well. Wash all the vegetables well, too.

The same brine is used for making all the pickles—cucumbers, turnips, or chilies—so be sure to make enough for the vegetables you're using. This recipe makes enough for 2 pounds (1kg) vegetables.

The beet in the turnip Kabis is optional to turn the pickles pink.

Pickles are essential in the Lebanese pantry. Their acidity brings a sharp contrast to a dish's other flavors.

1. Make the brine. In a large saucepan over medium-high heat, bring the water, vinegar, salt, and sugar to a boil, and cook until the sugar and salt are dissolved. Remove from the heat, and allow the brine to cool.

2. Arrange your choice of vegetables in canning jars. Add the garlic and spice, as appropriate, and fill the jars with the cooled brine. Be sure all the vegetables are submerged.

3. Tightly close the jars, place them in the pantry or refrigerator, and let pickle for at least 48 hours. The flavor intensifies after a week.

Kashta

LEBANESE CLOTTED CREAM

PREP TIME: **5 MINUTES**
+ overnight (chilling)

COOK TIME: **30 MINUTES**

TOTAL TIME: **35 MINUTES**
+ chilling

MAKES: about 3 cups (690g)

ingredients:

2 qt (1.8 liters) cold whole milk, divided

¼ cup (60ml) white vinegar

½ cup (50g) corn flour

¼ cup (50g) sugar

⅓ cup (75ml) cream

1 tbsp **Maa al Ward (Rose Water; page 244)**

1 tbsp orange blossom water

storage:

Store in an airtight container in the refrigerator for up to 3 days, or freeze for up to 2 months. Defrost in the refrigerator before using. Do not refreeze.

note:

Kashta is used in many recipes, but you can eat it separately, too. Enjoy it cold with a drizzle of honey, or garnish with rose jam or Kater (Sugar Syrup; page 252).

Kashta is a much-loved creamy Lebanese dessert. It's also the main ingredient in many traditional Lebanese sweets.

1. In a large pot over medium-low heat, bring 6 cups (1.4 liters) milk to an almost boil, stirring constantly. Turn off the heat, and add the vinegar, stirring gently but continuously. As curds form, use a slotted spoon to transfer them to a sieve to strain and cool.

2. In a pot, dissolve the corn flour in ½ cup (125ml) cold milk. Add the rest of the milk, sugar, and cream, set over medium heat, and cook, stirring, for 10 to 15 minutes or until the mixture thickens. Remove from the heat and set aside to cool for a few minutes. Add the curds, Maa al Ward, and orange blossom water, and stir to incorporate.

3. Transfer to an airtight container, and place in the refrigerator overnight. Stir well before using.

Toum

GARLIC SAUCE

| PREP TIME: **15 MINUTES** | COOK TIME: **NONE** | TOTAL TIME: **15 MINUTES** |

MAKES: 3 cups (690g)

VEGAN

GLUTEN FREE

ingredients:

3–4 heads garlic (173g), peeled

½ tbsp salt

3 cups (750ml) vegetable or another neutral oil, divided

½ cup (125ml) freshly squeezed lemon juice

storage:

The sauce will be better if you allow it to marinate and "set" in the refrigerator for at least 2 or 3 hours before serving. Store any leftovers in an airtight container in the refrigerator for up to 3 days.

note:

Fresh mint leaves are a popular addition to this sauce.

This Lebanese garlic sauce is thick, creamy, and packed with garlic flavor. It's a great dip for grilled chicken, chicken shawarma, and shish tawook.

1. In a food processor, purée the garlic and salt to a smooth paste.

2. With the machine still running, begin to add the oil. Slowly add 1 tablespoon at a time, allowing time between each spoonful for the oil to fully incorporate.

3. After you've added the first few tablespoons of oil, begin alternating between adding the oil and adding about 1 tablespoon lemon juice.

4. If the food processor starts to get warm, pause the process and turn off the machine. The heat can cause the emulsification to break.

5. Continue processing, adding any remaining oil and lemon juice, until the mixture emulsifies and you have a thick, creamy sauce.

Awarma

MEAT PRESERVE

PREP TIME: **5 MINUTES**	COOK TIME: **40 MINUTES**	TOTAL TIME: **45 MINUTES**

MAKES: 1 large jar

GLUTEN FREE

ingredients:

2 cups (400g) lamb fat (leyah), diced small

1 lb (500g) minced/ground meat (beef or lamb)

1 bay leaf

½ tbsp salt

1 tsp black pepper

½ tbsp **Lebanese 7 Spices (page 261)**

storage:

Store in the refrigerator for up to 1 year.

Awarma is a preserved Levantine ground beef our ancestors made to preserve meat when refrigeration wasn't available.

1. In a saucepan over medium-low heat, add the diced lamb fat, and melt, stirring occasionally, for 15 to 20 minutes or until the fat is completely melted.

2. Using a fine sieve, strain the melted fat to remove any small unmelted bits.

3. Pour most of the rendered fat into a clean, sterilized, dry glass jar, leaving a little in the pan to fry the minced meat.

4. Add the minced meat to the pan along with the bay leaf, salt, pepper, and Lebanese 7 Spices, and cook for about 25 minutes.

5. Remove the bay leaf. Ladle the cooked meat into the jar with the melted fat. Set aside to cool completely before closing the jar.

Tahini

SESAME PASTE

MAKES: 2 cups (510g)

VEGAN

GLUTEN FREE

ingredients:

3⅔ cups (510g) sesame seeds

½ tsp salt

storage:

Store in a glass container in the pantry or the refrigerator for up to 3 months.

note:

The separation of the oils over time is natural. Simply stir the Tahini before you use it.

Tahini, or sesame paste, is known for being an ingredient in hummus, but its uses go far beyond that. It's also an amazing alternative to nut butters.

1. In a medium pan over low heat, toast the sesame seeds for about 5 minutes or until they're fragrant. Be sure to stir constantly so the seeds on the bottom don't burn.

2. In a high-speed food processor or blender, process the toasted seeds and salt until the sauce reaches a consistency you like. The longer you blend, the smoother and runnier it will be. I like mine very smooth, so I blend it for about 7 minutes, turning off the machine about halfway through so it doesn't overheat.

Taratur

TAHINI SAUCE

PREP TIME: **10 MINUTES**	COOK TIME: **NONE**	TOTAL TIME: **10 MINUTES**

MAKES: 1 cup (230g)

VEGAN

GLUTEN FREE

ingredients:

½ cup (113g) **Tahini (Sesame Paste; page 250)**

2 cloves garlic (6g), minced

Juice of 1 large lemon

½ cup (125ml) water plus more as needed

1 tsp salt

Fresh flat-leaf parsley

Lemon wedges

storage:

Store in an airtight container in the refrigerator for up to 3 days.

note:

You can add ½ teaspoon cumin, or more if you like, especially if you plan on using this for fish recipes.

Taratur takes Tahini to the next level. It's great as a dip, especially for fish recipes, and is an essential sauce served with falafel and beef shawarma.

1. In a medium bowl, whisk together the Tahini, garlic, lemon juice, water, and salt until the sauce has a smooth texture. If the mixture is still too thick, add a bit more water.

2. If serving as a dip, garnish with parsley and serve with lemon wedges for squeezing.

Kater

SUGAR SYRUP

PREP TIME: **5 MINUTES**	COOK TIME: **5 MINUTES**	TOTAL TIME: **10 MINUTES**

MAKES: 1 cup (250ml)

VEGAN

GLUTEN FREE

ingredients:

1 cup (200g) sugar

½ cup (125ml) water

1 tsp freshly squeezed lemon juice

½ tsp **Maa al Ward (Rose Water; page 244)** (optional)

½ tsp orange blossom water (optional)

storage:

Store in the glass bottle in the refrigerator for several weeks.

Kater is one of the essential recipes served with most Arabic sweets. Some dessert dishes require a complete soak of warm Kater before being served.

1. In a small saucepan over medium heat, combine the sugar and water. Bring to a boil, stirring to dissolve the sugar, and cook for 4 or 5 minutes or until the sugar is all dissolved.

2. Add the lemon juice, remove from the heat, and stir in the Maa al Ward (if using) and the orange blossom water (if using).

3. Cool completely, and store in a glass bottle.

Debs al Romman

POMEGRANATE MOLASSES

PREP TIME: **40 MINUTES** | COOK TIME: **40 MINUTES** | TOTAL TIME: **1 HOUR 20 MINUTES**

MAKES: 12 tablespoons

VEGAN

GLUTEN FREE

This sweet-and-sour pomegranate reduction is used in a variety of Middle Eastern, African, and Persian dishes and something I enjoyed a lot of growing up in Lebanon. It's easy to make and can be added to a variety of sweet as well as savory dishes.

ingredients:

5 large pomegranates

½ cup (125ml) freshly squeezed lemon juice

REMOVE THE POMEGRANATE SEEDS:

1. Carefully cut the top ⅓ part of the pomegranate's skin. Make a circular incision around the flower-like petals on top of the fruit (the calyx) and then make 5 or 6 incisions downward, toward the bottom of the fruit. Remove the calyx.

2. Using your fingers, press in the center of the fruit, over the fleshy white part, and pull apart the pomegranate toward the cuts you made. It will open like a flower.

3. Turn the open pomegranate down over a large bowl, and hit the bottom of the fruit a few times with a big wooden spoon. This will make all the seeds come out into the bowl. Repeat with the remaining pomegranates.

4. Fill the bowl with water. The seeds will stay at the bottom, and any pieces of the white flesh will float to the top where you can collect and remove them with a spoon. Drain the water.

JUICE THE POMEGRANATE SEEDS:

1. With the seeds still in the large bowl, use a handheld blender to crush and mash the seeds into a watery purée.

2. Using a fine-mesh strainer, strain out the liquid, pressing on the mashed seeds to extract every drop of juice.

MAKE THE DEBS AL ROMMAN:

1. In a large pot over medium heat, add the pomegranate and lemon juices. Bring to a soft boil, reduce the heat to low, and simmer, stirring occasionally, for 30 to 40 minutes or until the juices have reduced to about ¼ the original volume.

2. When you see thick, viscous bubbles, or when the molasses coats the back of a spoon, remove it from the heat.

3. Allow to cool completely before transferring to an airtight sterilized glass bottle and storing it in a cool, dark place.

storage:

If you're not juicing the pomegranate seeds right away, you can store them in an airtight container in the refrigerator for up to 7 days, or freeze for up to 3 months. Same with the juice: if not using right away, store in a glass bottle in the refrigerator for up to 5 days. Store the Debs al Romman in an airtight container in the pantry or refrigerator for up to 6 months.

notes:

If you don't have a handheld blender, you can use a regular blender to crush the seeds.

If you have a nut milk bag, you can use it to squeeze the juice from the crushed seeds instead of straining it.

Kishik

POWDERED FERMENTED YOGURT & WHEAT

PREP TIME: **7–11 DAYS**	COOK TIME: **NONE**	TOTAL TIME: **7–11 DAYS**

MAKES: 9 cups (1kg)

ingredients:

14¼ cups (4kg) cow's milk yogurt, or mixture of cow's milk yogurt and goat's milk yogurt, divided

2⅔ cups (500g) white coarse bulgur, washed, drained well, and dried

⅓ cup (96g) salt, divided

storage:

Store in an airtight container in a cool, dry place for up to 1 year.

notes:

Dry the washed bulgur in a sunny, airy spot for a few days. If you have a dehydrator, it can dry the bulgur. (It can also dry the bulgur for 12 hours on the second and third days.) If you're using homemade bulgur made from the Bulgur Wheat (Crushed Wheat; page 242) recipe, you can skip washing it.

For a more sour Kishik, repeat the process an extra time, adding ⅓ of the Labneh and ⅓ of the salt each time.

Kishik is a delicious preserved Lebanese dairy product made with wheat and yogurt.

1. In a large bowl, mix 3½ cups (1kg) yogurt with the bulgur. Cover with a cotton cloth, and let soak at room temperature overnight.

2. Make Labneh (Strained Yogurt; page 16) with the rest of the yogurt.

3. On the second day, rub the bulgur by hand to ensure it has absorbed the yogurt. Mix in ½ of the Labneh and ½ of the salt. Spread the mixture on cotton sheets, and dry in the sun for 3 to 5 days. Rub the kishik between your palms to break it into smaller pieces and accelerate the drying process.

4. After 3 to 5 days, repeat step 3 with the remaining Labneh and salt, ferment in the sun for 3 to 5 more days, and rub daily.

5. When the kishik is fully dry, grind it to a fine powder.

Kamouneh

GREEN BULGUR MIX

PREP TIME: **10 MINUTES**	COOK TIME: **NONE**	TOTAL TIME: **10 MINUTES**

MAKES: 2 cups (440g)

VEGAN

ingredients:

1 cup (12g) fresh mint leaves

1 cup (10g) fresh basil leaves

¼ cup (5g) fresh marjoram, or 1 tsp dried if fresh is unavailable

½ cup (7g) fresh flat-leaf parsley leaves

½ cup (55g) spring onion

½ cup (125g) white onion

1 large hot green chili pepper

¼ peel from 1 medium orange (13g)

1 cup (150g) fine **Bulgur Wheat (Crushed Wheat; page 242)**

½ tsp salt

3 tbsp **Kamouneh Spice Blend (page 264)**

storage:

Store in the refrigerator for up to up to 1 week, or freeze for up to 3 months.

This aromatic mixture serves as a base ingredient in all sorts of kibbeh and the Kamounit Banadoura (Tomatoes with Bulgur; page 170). The flavor-enhancing secret ingredient is the orange peel!

1. In a food processor, add the mint, basil, marjoram, parsley, spring onion, white onion, hot green chili pepper, and orange peel. In a second layer, add the Bulgur Wheat, salt, and Kamouneh Spice Blend. Process for 3 minutes, stopping occasionally to scrape down the sides, until everything is finely chopped and well blended.

2. Transfer the Kamouneh mix to an airtight glass container.

note:

You can also spread the blended mixture on a large baking sheet and dry it in a sunny place, or dehydrate it in a dehydrator. The dried blend can be stored in a glass container in the pantry.

Makdous
PICKLED EGGPLANT

PREP TIME: **20 MINUTES** + 10–14 days (pickling)	COOK TIME: **10 MINUTES**	TOTAL TIME: **30 MINUTES** + pickling

MAKES: 1 large jar

VEGAN

GLUTEN FREE

Makdous is a staple appetizer in Levantine and Middle Eastern kitchens. This traditional olive oil–cured stuffed eggplant is perfect for breakfast or as a side dish with other mezze.

ingredients:

2 lb (1kg) baby eggplant (about 20)

2 tbsp salt, divided

4.5 oz (125g) red chili pepper, seeds removed, and finely chopped

2 heads garlic (60g), peeled and mashed

2 cups (190g) walnuts, roughly chopped or ground

Olive oil

storage:

If you keep them in the oil, completely covered, the Makdous can keep for up to 1 year. No need to refrigerate; just store at room temperature in the pantry because the olive oil acts as a natural preservative.

1. In a large saucepan, add the eggplants and water to cover. Bring to a boil over medium-high heat, and cook for 5 to 10 minutes to soften. Turn off the heat, and let them sit in the water for 10 to 15 minutes. Drain.

2. Cut the tops off the eggplants. Carefully slice the eggplants halfway through lengthwise, like a book, and rub some salt on the inside of each. Arrange the eggplants on a drying rack, not touching, and press with a heavy object. Set aside overnight to extract as much water as possible.

3. Add the chili peppers to a sieve, and press out all the excess liquid. Transfer to a bowl, add the garlic and walnuts, and mix well. Stuff the eggplants with about 1 tablespoon of the mixture, depending on their size.

4. In a clean, sterilized glass jar, carefully stack the eggplants so the stuffing won't fall out. Sprinkle the top liberally with salt, and fill the jar with olive oil. Be sure all the eggplants are entirely covered, and close the jar tightly.

5. Set the jar in a cool, dark place for 10 to 14 days before eating. If during that time you notice the olive oil isn't entirely covering the eggplants, add more oil.

Za'atar

WILD OREGANO MIX

PREP TIME: **5 MINUTES**	COOK TIME: **5 MINUTES**	TOTAL TIME: **10 MINUTES**

MAKES: about 2¼ cups (200g)

VEGAN

GLUTEN FREE

ingredients:

½ cup (78g) sesame seeds, toasted

¾ cup (78g) dried oregano, ground

½ cup (38g) ground sumac

½ tbsp salt

note:

If you only have fresh oregano, you can dry it for use in Za'atar. Rinse and pat dry the stems, arrange on a baking sheet lined with parchment paper, and dehydrate in a 105°F (40°C) oven for 3 or 4 hours, checking after 2 hours. If your oven doesn't go that low, dehydrate in a 165°F (75°C) oven for about 1 hour, checking after 30 or 40 minutes and then every 5 to 10 minutes after until the leaves feel dry and crumble easily. Cool the dried oregano completely, remove the leaves from the stems, and grind the leaves to a fine powder. If you have a dehydrator, you can use it instead.

This earthy, herby Lebanese spice blend is used in a variety of dishes. It's great mixed with olive oil and spread on Markouk (Paper Thin Bread; page 238) or Manakish (Breakfast Pies; page 12).

1. In a small, dry pan (no oil) over medium heat, toast the sesame seeds, stirring constantly so the seeds don't burn, for 4 or 5 minutes. Remove from the heat, and cool completely.

2. In a bowl, combine the oregano, sumac, toasted sesame seeds, and salt.

3. Store in an airtight glass container in a cool, dry place.

storage:

This will last up to 1 year if stored in an airtight glass container in a cool, dark place. Or freeze for 1 year or more.

Lebanese 7 Spices

PREP TIME: **5 MINUTES**	COOK TIME: **5 MINUTES**	TOTAL TIME: **10 MINUTES**

MAKES: about 3½ tablespoons

VEGAN

GLUTEN FREE

ingredients:

1 tbsp allspice berries

1 medium cinnamon stick (or 1 tbsp ground cinnamon)

½ tbsp black peppercorns

½ tsp whole cloves (or ground)

1 tsp ground ginger

½ tsp freshly grated nutmeg

½ tsp mahlab (optional)

storage:

This will last for up to 6 months or more if stored in an airtight glass container in a cook, dark place, but aim to use within 3 months for the best flavor.

This popular Lebanese spice blend can dramatically alter a dish's flavor, with its distinctive sweet aroma and hint of bitter.

1. In a small, dry (no oil) skillet over medium-low heat, toast the whole allspice berries, cinnamon stick, peppercorns, and cloves, stirring constantly, for 2 or 3 minutes or until the spices begin to pop and smell fragrant. Remove from the heat, and cool completely.

2. Using a spice grinder, grind the toasted spices to a powder. Sieve the mixture for a fine powder, and regrind any larger pieces.

3. Add the ginger, nutmeg, and mahlab (if using), and mix.

4. Store in an airtight glass container or spice jar. Shake well before each use.

Falafel Spice

MAKES: ¼ cup (90g)

VEGAN

GLUTEN FREE

ingredients:

2 tbsp coriander seeds (or ground coriander)

1 tbsp cumin seeds (or ground cumin)

½ tbsp black peppercorns (or ground pepper)

1 medium cinnamon stick (or 1 tsp ground cinnamon)

1 tsp red chili powder

note:

If you're using the ground version of some or all of the spices, measure them into a bowl, mix, and then transfer them to a glass container or spice jar.

storage:

Store in an airtight glass container in a cool, dark place for up to 1 year.

This rich, aromatic, earthy spice blend gives Falafel (page 160) its signature flavor.

1. In a small, dry (no oil) skillet over medium-low heat, toast the whole coriander seeds, cumin seeds, black peppercorns, and the cinnamon stick, stirring constantly, for 2 or 3 minutes or until the spices smell fragrant. Remove from the heat, and cool completely.

2. Using a spice grinder, grind the toasted spices to a powder. Sieve the mixture for a fine powder, and regrind any larger pieces.

3. Add the chili powder, and mix.

4. Store in an airtight glass container or spice jar. Shake well before each use.

Kabsi Spice Blend

PREP TIME: **5 MINUTES**	COOK TIME: **5 MINUTES**	TOTAL TIME: **10 MINUTES**

MAKES: ½ cup (60g)
VEGAN
GLUTEN FREE

ingredients:

2 tbsp coriander seeds

1 tbsp cumin seeds

½ tbsp black peppercorns

½ tsp white peppercorns

½ tbsp fennel seeds

1 tsp whole cloves

1 cinnamon stick

3 black cardamom pods

4 green cardamom pods

1 dried black lime

½ tsp red chili powder

¼ tsp ground ginger

¼ tsp ground turmeric

storage:

Store in an airtight glass container
in a cool, dark place for up to 1 year.

Kabsi Spice Blend is an essential seasoning mixture that gives Kabsi rice its distinct flavor.

1. In a small, dry (no oil) skillet over medium-low heat, toast the whole coriander seeds, cumin seeds, black and white peppercorns, fennel seeds, cloves, cinnamon stick, black and green cardamom pods, and black lime, stirring constantly, for 2 or 3 minutes or until the spices smell fragrant. Remove from the heat, and cool completely.

2. Using a spice grinder, grind the toasted spices to a powder. Sieve the mixture for a fine powder, and regrind any larger pieces.

3. Add the chili powder, ginger, and turmeric; mix.

4. Store in an airtight glass container or spice jar. Shake well before each use.

Kamouneh Spice Blend

PREP TIME: **5 MINUTES**	COOK TIME: **5 MINUTES**	TOTAL TIME: **10 MINUTES**

MAKES: 1⅔ cups (150g)

VEGAN

GLUTEN FREE

ingredients:

5 tbsp cumin seeds

½ tbsp black peppercorns

½ tbsp allspice berries

1 whole nutmeg

¼ tsp whole cloves

2 cinnamon sticks

2 tbsp dried Damask rose
(*Rosa damascene*) petals

1 tbsp sweet paprika

½ tsp dried red chili pepper

1 tbsp dried marjoram

1 tbsp dried basil

1 tbsp dried mint

½ tsp salt

Authentic Kamouneh Spice is from southern Lebanon and gives dishes an earthy taste. This is from the deep south of Lebanon, from my mother, an expert at making it with the best, freshest taste.

1. In a small, dry (no oil) skillet over medium-low heat, toast the cumin seeds, black peppercorns, allspice, nutmeg, cloves, and cinnamon sticks, stirring constantly, for 2 or 3 minutes or until the spices smell fragrant. Remove from the heat, and cool completely.

2. Using a spice grinder, grind the toasted spices and the rose petals, sweet paprika, red chili pepper, marjoram, basil, mint, and salt to a medium-fine powder.

3. Store in an airtight glass container or spice jar in a cool, dark place for up to 1 or 2 years. Shake well before each use.

Shawarma Spice

MAKES: 6⅔ tablespoons

VEGAN

GLUTEN FREE

ingredients:

1½ tbsp allspice berries

1½ tbsp black peppercorns

14 cardamom pods

½ tsp whole cloves

1 cinnamon stick (or ½ tbsp ground cinnamon)

½ tsp grated nutmeg

½ tbsp ground ginger

1 tsp ground sumac

½ tsp ground mahlab

½ tsp citric acid

storage:

Store in an airtight glass container in a cool, dark place for up to 4 or 5 months.

Shawarma Spice is an essential ingredient in Lebanese cooking. It's used to season all kinds of shawarma beef, lamb, and chicken.

1. In a small, dry (no oil) skillet over medium-low heat, toast the allspice, black peppercorns, cardamom pods, cloves, and cinnamon stick, stirring constantly, for 2 or 3 minutes or until the spices smell fragrant. Remove from the heat, and cool completely.

2. Using a spice grinder, grind the toasted spices to a powder. Sieve the mixture for a fine powder, and regrind any larger pieces.

3. Add the nutmeg, ginger, sumac, mahlab, and citric acid, and mix.

4. Store in an airtight glass container or spice jar. Shake well before each use.

Acknowledgments

I would like to dedicate this work to my mom and dad, for their unconditional love and support. I would also like to thank my family and my close friends, Oliver, Zarry, and Clark, for all their help and support. A special thanks to my beloved sister, Rehab, for her invaluable input and encouragement.

About the Author

Samira Kazan is an award-winning food blogger, recipe developer, and influencer with boundless passion and instant attraction to colorful, vibrant, and healthy things. Samira loves creating delicious, rainbow-inspired, often plant-based recipes and shares her fresh and flavorful Middle Eastern recipes on her blog, Alphafoodie.com, and on social media. Samira is a Netflix/Channel 4 *Crazy Delicious* winner; has hosted international workshops for brands like Google, Pinterest, and Duty-Free; was featured on Bored Panda online and in *Vogue, Time,* and *Evening Standard;* and was on the cover of *Artful Living,* among others. Samira's Lebanese background, along with her travels throughout the country, consulting with top chefs and elders, have inspired her to collect and share the amazing tips, best practices, and authentic and traditional Lebanese recipes in this book.